# I WANNA
# HEAR HIM SAY,
# 'WELL DONE'

STEVE JOHNSON

# I WANNA HEAR HIM SAY, 'WELL DONE'

*Instead of going to hell
and gettin' burned well done*

DPI

DISCIPLESHIP
PUBLICATIONS
INTERNATIONAL

**I Wanna Hear Him Say, 'Well Done'**
©1999 by Discipleship Publications International
One Merrill Street, Woburn, MA 01801

All Scripture quotations, unless indicated, are taken from
the NEW INTERNATIONAL VERSION.
Copyright ©1973, 1978, 1984 by the International Bible Society.
Used by permission of Zondervan Publishing House.
All rights reserved.

The "NIV" and "New International Version" trademarks
are registered in the United States Patent Trademark Office
by the International Bible Society.
Use of either trademark requires the permission of
the International Bible Society.

Printed in the United States of America

*Cover design: Chris Costello*
*Image of New York City ©1999 PhotoDisc*

ISBN: 1-57782-119-X

*I'm dedicating this book, the first book I've ever written in my life, to Russ Ewell. I really ought to dedicate it to my mom, or my wife, or Kip McKean, since he's the closest thing to a boss I've ever had, but I'm going to bestow this honor on Russ because he's the one person most to blame for this book's existence—other than me, of course.*

*Russ introduced me to computers and cyberspace and all that jazz, and I can think of no one in our circle of friends who deserves more credit for instigating the use of these machines in our fellowship than he does.*

*I remember Russ, first as a Boston University kid, then as the evangelist for the D.C. church eons ago, pounding away at a keyboard, staring into a monitor's screen, all the while trying to explain to me how these marvels were "the future." Well, more than any other generation perhaps, we've come to enjoy our future during our own lifetimes.*

*I love Russ, in spite of all the work he's inspired me to do. And I admire him for his ministry, his family and the fact that his passions always progress the work of the Lord. The man's been dealt some rough cards in his time, but thanks to God, he's playing 'em well. Very well.*

# Contents

# Foreword

I have figured out who Steve Johnson is to the Kingdom of God—at least part of who he is: Will Rogers. "I never met a man I didn't like," the sage from Oklahoma often said. And he had a way of making folks laugh at him, others and themselves in a way that left them humbled but not humiliated.

The quality of gentleness or "sweet reasonableness"—as I have heard the Greek scholars translate it—rarely lauded, infrequently urged upon us, but desperately needed—how gloriously it is demonstrated in Steve's life and demeanor. I don't know where we would be without him, and I hope the Lord agrees with me that we don't need to find out for a long, long time. We are about the most serious business in the world, but somehow we need to take ourselves less seriously, in a holy kind of way. I know of no one who helps us better see how to do that than our brother Steve.

Steve has written a book that is just as unique as he is. Part history, part theology, part common sense, it is the story of a man and a movement all rolled into one. In its history, it puts a human face on events that many of us have only heard about and perhaps view with a sense of mystery and reverence. In its theology, it helps us grasp the concepts of faith, sin, righteousness and grace (and many others) on a down-to-earth level. In its common sense...well, that part just speaks for itself.

The thing about Steve Johnson is that you know that whatever else you are getting, you are getting the truth as he sees it and the story as he saw it, without pretense, pomp and pride. And in a day when so many of the famous preachers and religious leaders in our world seem a bit more like game show hosts than men of God, Steve is a refreshingly real alternative. He is a genuine preacher, leader and writer because he is a genuine human being, and that is what makes this book so valuable. Sit back in your favorite easy chair, or out on the back porch, and read it. Take your time. Read some; put it down; come back; read some more later. Or read it all at once if you've a mind to. Steve won't mind; he'll just be glad you spent some time with him. Laugh, cry, think and learn. And after you have read this book, you will see that you have learned far more than you first realized and that you are more likely to hear the words "well done" from the Lord because you did.

Steve, my friend, keep on loving life, your family, the kingdom, the King and all the king's men. You have given far more to all of our lives than you, I or any of us know. But the Lord does know, and I have a feeling he is very happy with you and what you do, but especially with all that you are.

*Sam Laing*
*Durham, North Carolina*

# Prologue

*Heaven's stories are Earth's most sacred writings. But what if the life you're leading is one of the stories we'll be reading in heaven?*

Here's the deal....

If you read this book from cover to cover, beginning to end, not skipping any pages, looking up all the hard words you don't understand, I promise you'll be smarter, thinner, sleep better, feel freer, learn how to get married if you're single, have a better sex life if you're married, grow cleaner kids and know some secrets about people that I probably shouldn't tell you.

You see, I'm not a theologian. Or a scholar. Sometimes I feel like I'm just an overactive imagination running amok in the kingdom of God. But maybe this time that can work to your advantage.

I get people all the time acting like if they could just spend an hour with a spiritual giant like me they would think they had already died and gone to heaven.

Well, okay. I'll risk popping that bubble. C'mon. Let's go! I'm gonna tell you a lot more than you asked for and probably more than you want to know. 'Cause all I care about is hearing him say, "Well done."

First time I said that little joke, which became the title of this book, was like all moments of genius. It just came to me, seemed like the thing to say, and like all true geniuses, I can't for the life of me remember who I stole it from. And this phrase became like a particular spice you like to use over and over in your favorite food. I'd throw it into the middle of a sermon to wake people up. I'd invent an extra point to an already too long message just so I could shoot it out there. But in time I realized that this wasn't just a cheap one-liner—it's the theme of my life. The only stuff I do that matters is the stuff I do because I want to go to heaven. I don't want to go to hell. I want God to like me, think I'm a neat guy and be proud he let the sperm and the egg meet up and make me. Obviously, this could be just another feel good, positive outlook, "ain't it great to be a Christian" booklet with a slightly witty title and less than clever author. But, no way am I going to let that happen.

I'm going to show those of you who doubt the existence of God that you're crazy as a coot. I'm going to show those of you who worry about whether or not you're going to heaven that you're spoiling a really good time and probably going to go to heaven anyway. And I'm going to do it just like we were sitting in my backyard, which I'll tell you about later. Sitting in my backyard, coupla' Bibles laying near us, kids playing on the swings and me yakking like we got all day. And maybe we do.

And chapters? We don't need no stinkin' chapters. I'm on a roll, and you just read as much as you want, then mark your place the best you can; come back later, I'll still be yakking. Today is my birthday. I'm forty-three and I've never written a book before. You're dealing with a rank amateur, so please be gracious.

A
♠

I believe that I'm absolutely the luckiest man alive. Now, the Biblical word that I ought to use is "blessed." That word in the New Testament is most often translated from a Greek word *makarios*, which is defined as "happy" or "fortunate" in all the Bible dictionaries you can look it up in. So to me, even though I don't superstitiously believe in luck, I think that saying I'm lucky is the best way I can express my appreciation to God for the incredible grace he has given me. Salvation would be enough, but the Lord has inexplicably seen fit to give an ordinary guy like me an extraordinary life. Like David said in his prayer, "Is this your usual way of dealing with man?" The generosity God has shown to me, demonstrated in experiences, relationships, opportunities and comforts, is way out of proportion to what I could ever possibly deserve.

Consequently, I believe that my existence better reflect appreciation, or I'm on dangerous ground.

So almost everything that I do is motivated by a desire to convince people that God is real, he loves us and wants us to be saved, stay saved and save others. That's my goal and these days you call such things "agendas."

Everyone has an agenda. It's not always conscious. Every thought and action is not carefully planned out by every individual every second of the day. But, we all want stuff.

We want our kids to be healthy.

We want our stomachs to be full—and flat at the same time.

We want to be liked, and we want to be financially independent.

And whether we know it or not, we're like sharks, always swimming around, looking for that next bite that will satisfy us, gratify us or pacify us until, well...the next bite. But few people ever figure out what God's agenda is and that what he wants for us is infinitely better than achieving our own finite agendas. So, making what we want the same as what he wants...well, that's the trick.

What does God want? Lots of "don'ts" come to mind. Don't smoke, don't cuss, don't get pregnant if you're not married and don't get married to a boy...if you're a boy. But the Bible reveals that if you *really* want to understand, *God is a loving Father who doesn't want us to get hurt.* The devil is an evil child abductor, and God is the fretting dad who doesn't want his kids to end up on a milk carton for all eternity. He grieves when we run away from home. He is absolutely sick with anxiety when we're stolen by evil. He mourns when we prefer the company of hoodlums over his presence and the thrill of cheap shenanigans over his agenda for our lives. And just like any of us with our own kids, he wants to be able to say, "Well done, good and faithful son, daughter, beloved of mine" more than we could ever comprehend.

My mother always said that I'd never understand how much she loved me until I had a child of my own. She was twenty years old when I was born in the back room of Dr. Stone's little office in minuscule Holly Grove, Arkansas. She and my dad weren't doing real well with each other at the time. Fact was, they had married before she finished her senior year of high school. She was a starter on the women's basketball team, a soprano in the chorus and loved school, but this truck-driving redneck two years her senior just wouldn't leave her alone. He wanted two things in life: (1) to escape a future of farming soybeans, and (2) HER.

So she gave in between semesters, mid-basketball season, and married at seventeen years of age. All of her friends assumed she was pregnant; however, she had a standard of faith that would not allow her to fool around before marriage—one of the reasons the boy was wooing her so hard. Three years later I was born, but not before he broke her heart, and she moved back home with her family. She found out he'd been cheating on her in the worst way and at the time didn't even know that she was pregnant. But when she realized that she had a baby coming, she was determined that the child would have a father, even if she didn't love him. Even if he'd destroyed her life.

She wasn't going to let anything destroy mine.

She kept this secret for thirty-four years, and over a lifetime I had no idea of the pain and scars, the unresolved hurt in my family because right or wrong, in this young, basketball-playing, singing, praying, cute-as-all-get-out brunette's mind, the only important thing was me going to heaven.

Whether she did or not.

My wife and I got married in 1977, and eleven years and one miscarriage later, our first child was born. My new little girl couldn't have been more than three weeks old when I, after rocking her to sleep in our tiny Manhattan apartment, laid her down ever so gently

*Me with my mom in the early going: "In this young, basketball-playing, singing, praying, cute-as-all-get-out brunette's mind, the only important thing was me going to heaven."*

and trance-like walked to the phone and called a fifty-four-year-old graying brunette to tell her, "Mom, I know what you meant now."

"Steve?"

I don't think she knew it, but I was crying.

"Thank you, Mom. I love you, Mom."

"Well...I love you, too, Steve. Always have."

"Oh, I know you do. Now I know you do."

We can't begin to understand the love of God until we see him as a father. Just a dad who wants to see his kids do well. Just a dad who knows that oo-oo baby, it's a wild world, a wild universe and he doesn't want us hurt or lost, alone, stranded, starving....

So here's a few things he did, like any good father, to try to smooth the road for us, even if we are going to drive as reckless as a diplomat with immunity. Some things he did, without cheating...'cause we have to do a lot of this ourselves or else we don't grow up right...so that he'd be able to say, "Well done. Good driving," instead of seeing us crash and burn in flames. Flames that never go out.

A
♥

God makes the stupidity of sin obvious even if we try to be oblivious.

James 4:17. Read it. And then you tell me why that verse is in that particular place. Let me give you the Steve Johnson paraphrased version:

*After all, what is a life like but a mist or a vapor that drifts through the air for a while and then vanishes? So if you know what is good to do and don't do it, you're sinning.*

For years, in my infantile approach to the Scriptures, I could never figure out why James, inspired by the Holy Spirit, whatever *that* means, chose to put this thought as the closing to a lecture on the brevity of life. But, it's really obvious. After explaining that we are like a mist that evaporates quickly, James says that if you know what's good for you, do it. Do it while you have the chance, 'cause you just may never have *another* chance. Our motto, with apologies to Nike, ought to be "Just *DONE* it." Don't put off doing what you know is right 'cause you might die real soon. Could happen. Definitely will happen sometime. But we don't really believe we're ever gonna die, so we procrastinate some really important stuff.

"Sin" wasn't always a religious word. We think of it now as the evil, filthy, wretched junk that put Jesus on the cross, and it's that and more. But originally, it was an archery term. "To sin" was "to err, to miss the mark." In Hebrew the word translated as "sin" is *hat'*. A really cool thing is that in Judges 20:16 you can read about 700 left-handed Benjamites and every one of them could "sling a stone at a hair...and not *miss*." The word that is here translated "miss" is the same word *hat'*, which again, means "missing, going astray, or missing the mark." The Greek New Testament uses the word *hamartia,* which has the same definition. The word "sin" that we use in English is the same as the Latin for "sin," which means "missing" in the sense of not having, as in "sincere," which means "without wax"—an interesting story in itself. When potters would try to sell pottery that had been cracked, perhaps inferior stuff that hadn't fired well, they would fill the cracks with wax. So, in time a commercial word evolved, "sincere," which was an advertisement for pottery *with no wax*. Nothing was covering the flaws. So, part of the evolution of the word that we think of as sin involves this idea of "not having." To err, to miss, to "not have a relationship with...."

Instead of thinking of sin as something God hates because he's offended by it, try imagining it as something God hates because it destroys his children.

We don't want our kids to touch poison ivy. I've spent a poor man's fortune on Round-Up® and a good deal of time trying to kill a backyard full of the stuff. I hate it and don't know what the Lord was thinking when he made it. If I could, I'd make it a law that anyone who sees a patch of it has to stop whatever they're doing and kill it. I tell my kids, "Leaflets three, let it be!" I make it a sin to touch the stuff. A sin, because it's an error that hurts you. Do I hate my children if they disobey me and touch it and get covered with hideous blisters because they momentarily thought to themselves, *I can touch this if I want to. I don't know why he gets all worked up about this*? No, I don't hate them, ever. EVER. I despise those horrid blisters on them, though. Now the difference in me and God is that while I willingly doctor my itching children, I resent having to.

"If you had just obeyed me," I tell them.

But, don't you see? God, without resentment, doctored our hideous, festered sins with the blood of his son, Jesus. He tells us not to sin because of the mess it makes of our lives, not because he's some omnipotent prude who capriciously chose a fun list of activities to outlaw. He made us and knows how we best function. If we're like the teenager in the car, he's the dad who gave us the keys and knows where the dangerous curves are. He knows all the bad spots. And not just the really dangerous stuff; heck, *he knows every pothole in the universe.*

If the damaging nature of sin isn't obvious at first, we need to consider the wisdom of just obeying God as a way to gain insight into reality. Here again, the people are usually divided between the religious who believe that you better just obey or you'll go to hell and those who think that obeying an invisible deity is like being a spiritual lemming: robotic, hypnotic, superstitious obeisance that is supported by an ignorant herd mentality. In John 7:16-17, Jesus offers another alternative, the equivalent of a thirty-day, money-back guarantee. He said (and I paraphrase):

> *My teachings are not of human invention, by me or anyone else. Anyone who will do what I teach*

*will find out for himself whether or not I'm making all of this up or if, indeed as I've told you, it all comes from God Almighty.*

If anyone wants to know if his teachings are from God or not, all they need to do is try them. Seems the Lord is confident that, if put into practice, his teachings will convince you themselves. The merit of trying to obey the Bible is found in the benefits reaped by practicing what it preaches.

If all men and women who had sex together were married to each other for life, almost no homeless, fatherless children would exist. What a bizarre notion. Where would anyone get an idea like that? From the one who made us. The Bible doesn't tell us not to have sex outside of marriage because it's cutting down the fun we could have. Look what society has reaped from the hedonistic outlook. The educated response to this kind of Bible-based logic is usually to say, "We're just more honest than our Eisenhower parents were." Yeah, immorality wasn't invented by Hugh Hefner; he just exploited it better than anyone else. But don't compare this generation to previous generations. Look at our problems and then look at the Bible. Is it any wonder that our country has more single mothers than any previous generation when we give monetary compensation to girls with children out of wedlock? Is it any wonder that our prisons are bursting with men who didn't have two parents "training them in the way they should go so that when they were old they would not depart from it"? When you live in a society that's been brainwashed into thinking at one moment SEX EQUALS LOVE and then the next that SEX IS JUST A BIOLOGICAL ACT, then Jesus' words in John 8:31-32 make even more sense. Do what he says. Then you'll know the truth. Then the truth sets you free.

*Again, the merits of obeying the Bible are clear when you acknowledge the benefits of simply doing what the Bible says.*

Philippians 2:3 says to do nothing out of selfish ambition or vain conceit but in humility to consider others better than yourself. Apply that to your husband or wife. That's challenging, yeah, and it will make you tired if you do it. And happy.

I love Marty Fuqua. He's a tough rascal. First time I met Marty we were in college. I was twenty years old, beard and all, and after a devotional on a Friday night in Charleston, Illinois, I was leaving and stopped to talk to someone. I innocently sat on the hood of a brand new, screaming-pumpkin-orange-red Road Runner.

Now, Marty was a wrestler that Kip McKean, the campus minister, had found out about. A kid whose family had dragged him to the Church of Christ most of his life, and was now off on his own in college. He was cruising along enjoying the bliss of college life, attempting few things more difficult than a reversal from a full nelson, when Kip found him and dragged him to this devotional. He wasn't the best tempered sort back then. And I didn't know I was sitting on his car.

Marty comes out of the house.

First thing he does is look at his car.

He does this John Wayne strut toward me, and in the most somber, if not deepest, voice I ever heard in my life says, "Get off the car."

That was it. I'd just met Marty Fuqua. He got in. Drove off. That was all he said. That was about all he said to me that semester.

But not too long after that, he got baptized. And before the spring semester was over, he had me over for dinner to reach out to me, because he had gone from being Mr. Bad Attitude to becoming my big brother in the Lord. He went on to be the toughest campus minister and then just the toughest evangelist I've ever known. He's epitomized "tough" for me for about twenty-three years now.

Marty Fuqua says that fatigue is a prerequisite for perseverance.

Who's gonna argue with Marty?

And look how much sense it makes.

You don't persevere when everything's going your way. You win money, get a promotion and date the girl of your dreams, you don't say, "Boy, I'm just persevering."

No, you say, "Life is great. I'm cruising. Bring on more of this good stuff."

Lose the money, get fired and the girl says, "Are you nuts? I want a man like Marty Fuqua—not you!" Then what do you do?

You gotta persevere.

When you're tired. Not when you're feeling good, rested. But when you're tired and flat busted.

Paul says in Romans 5:3 that perseverance is a prerequisite for character. If we're not willing to work through the hard times when we're tired, then we are without character. My personal definition for character is simple: You have character if you NEVER QUIT.

And know that God is patient. Even when we're throwing tantrums, he loves us and will forgive us, if we'll just not disappear on him. Remember, the blisters he hates, the blistered he always loves.

My three year old swiped a pair of fingernail clippers from her mother's purse and was sneaking upstairs. Lisa caught her, but not before she put the clippers behind her back.

"What do you have?" Lisa asked.

"Nothing, Mommy."

Lying is a corporal offense in our family, and Lisa quickly resolved the matter. Then I came in.

"Tell your daddy what happened," Lisa said.

Skylar just shook her head no.

"Skylar, you have to obey Mommy; now tell me what happened."

"I don't want to," Skylar stonewalled.

So, a second offense in less than thirty minutes, but even after the punishment, she's still holding out. By this time Lisa has already filled me in on the dastardly fingernail clippers theft, and I'm only too anxious to put this heinous crime in the family closet, full of skeletons. But Skylar won't give an inch.

"Honey, I know what you did, I just want you to tell me so we can go on and have a great time together today. Tell me what you did."

"No, I don't want to."

So I pulled out the only other punishment in my arsenal at the moment.

"Okay, young lady, you are in time-out. You stand right there in the middle of the floor with your hands by your sides until I tell you that you can move."

So Lisa and I sit and talk as if we don't have a mutinous three-year-old in the middle of the room. In about five minutes she speaks.

"Daddy…"

"Yes?"

"I'm ready to tell you what happened."

Now, you have to out-think three year olds from every angle. You'd think that would be easy for a college-educated adult, but the truth is, both of our brains were scrambling during that five-minute time-out. She, figuring out that if she told me what happened *when she wanted to*, she could still claim victory. To be fair, my challenge was much harder because I had to figure what she figured and devise a strategy to counter her move. I was up to the task. In a rare moment of parental brilliance I said:

"So, you're ready to tell me?"

"Yes, Daddy," she said this with all the love and affection of a manipulating child who knows Daddy can be wrapped around her finger in a skinny minute.

"Well, there's just one problem."

She looked confused for a moment. I knew I had her.

"I'm not ready to hear you tell me what happened. You have to stay in time-out until I *allow* you to tell me."

Her jaw dropped but she stayed put, and a few minutes later, with the confidence of a deft chess master, I put down the newspaper I was holding upside down in front of my face, and told her to come over to me. "Okay, Skylar, tell me now what happened."

"I took Mommy's things that you cut your fingers with. I'm sorry. And I'm sorry I didn't tell you."

"I love you, baby."

"I love you, Daddy."

I held her on my lap for a lot longer than that time-out had lasted, and somewhere in there she looked up at me. "Daddy?"

"Uh-huh."

"Are we still buddies?"

"Of course we are, honey. We're always buddies; we'll always be buddies. Did you think Daddy wasn't your buddy just because I had to punish you like that?"

It had been the biggest ordeal over lying we'd ever had with her, but I was starting to realize the other things her little mind was scrambling over in the thick of the battle. She snuggled up tight against my chest.

"I love you, Daddy."

"Honey, I love you, too. I always love you."

Then I pulled her in front of my face, nose to nose.

"Don't you know that even when you were standing over there in the middle of the floor and wouldn't obey Daddy, I was still loving you. I never stop loving you. Even when you disobey me…I still love you."

She smiled and squeezed me tighter, and then I realized the lesson in what I said was as much for me as for her.

God doesn't stop loving us when we disobey. He doesn't turn his love on and off, even when we're in a *spiritual time-out*. He doesn't start loving us when we repent, as if we become such spiritually pure people that we deserve his love. We never deserve it and he never refrains from feeling it toward us. He was loving us even when we were messing up. And when we were messing up, we were damaging ourselves needlessly. Because God makes sin obvious, if we will only obey him.

So God only wants what's good for me. Fine. But what does THE CHURCH want? For many people their feeling is, "I can handle God, but not church!" We can handle the creator of the universe, but not each other?

"I'm just not into 'organized' religion."

So, you're into "disorganized" religion?

Look, I know what's really going on here. This is most of the real reason why I wanted to write this stuff down. You see, I believe that (1) there are lots of people outside the church right now whose main obstacle to becoming part of the church is fear; and (2) there are lots of people in the church right now whose main obstacle to staying in the church is anger.

Two of the main problems that will face any church that tries to strictly adhere to the model of Christianity set out in the Bible is that those outside the church will, at their most critical level, consider the church a cult; and those inside the church will, at their most critical level, consider the church a failure.

In 1976 I was a transfer student to a small state college in eastern Illinois. Ten thousand students set out in a small Midwest town, smack dab in the middle of a cornfield, and that's where I met the "DUDE." Kip McKean was my campus minister at the tiny congregation where I attended faithfully. But he was like no minister I had ever met in my life. Most minister guys I knew were happy if you just *came.* Kip actually expected you to *do something.* He was the first person to ever "get in my face" with the Bible. Now, my first reaction was not too much unlike an unwilling draftee when the drill sergeant gets in his face for the first time. Not that there was yelling and screaming going on.

"So, Steve. How are things going for you, spiritually?"

"Just fine, Kip. How are things going *for you,* spiritually?"

Then he sat there looking at me, and I looked right back at him, smiling.

This was a typical counseling appointment for Kip and me for the first nine months that I knew him. But during that time I stood idly by and watched as Kip

*"Kip McKean [here in about 1978] was my campus minister at the tiny congregation where I attended faithfully. But he was like no minister I had ever met in my life."*

almost single-handedly turned that tiny congregation into the biggest, baptizingest campus church in America, and it was in the middle of nowhere. Three hundred cynical, agnostic, Allman Brothers listening, Frisbee throwing college kids got baptized in less than two years, with over ninety percent staying faithful at least during their college years. I'd never seen such a thing.

Neither had the other religious organizations on campus. They weren't too happy because some of their constituents changed sides during that time. And then the bomb dropped, and the church franchise wars were never to be the same.

On November 18, 1978, in the jungles of Guyana, a drugged-up mass murderer changed the terminology that would be used for the rest of this century. Jim Jones, drugged, delusional and doctrinally corrupt, passed out the Kool Aid and poisoned his flock, introducing "cult" as a scare word that would be used for the rest of this millennium to smear any group or organization. With one word you could summon the images of dead, bloated bodies in that South American jungle, and apply it to your target. A religious group on campus believes you have to be baptized as part of the salvation plan? Call them a cult, and suddenly their Friday night devotionals are probably People's

Temple-like rituals preparing for mass suicide. And their Communion on Sunday? You really want to drink *that cult's* grape juice or eat *their* crackers?

Kip was walking across campus, toward the little church building where his office was after an evangelistic group Bible study in one of the dorms. We used to call those meetings "Soul Talks," an early seventies idea. And if Soul Talks weren't invented by the Crossroads Church of Christ down in Gainesville at the University of Florida, then surely no one used it any better or promoted it more than they did.

This particular night, as Kip passed the last dorm on the edge of the campus, a high rise six or seven stories tall, a kid yelled out of an upper floor window, "Hey, you down there! Hey, Jim Jones!"

That stung Kip for a long time. I think he was always prepared to be persecuted. But no one wants to be compared to a nut like Jim Jones.

Goes to show...we don't always get to choose our persecutions—they choose us.

The Sanhedrin didn't take Jesus to Pilate and say, "This is a real good guy trying to save the lost and set things right, and we're just a corrupt bunch of hypocrites who want him DEAD!"

Heck, no. They called him a blasphemer. That was a mean accusation around about AD 33. And calling a dedicated twenty-four-year-old minister "Jim Jones" was mean in 1978.

So, call a church a cult. Never mind the real issues.

In those days the campus ministries of the Churches of Christ were just about the only places you'd find much happening. You had the bus ministries, where churches would knock doors and invite kids to Sunday School and pick 'em up on Sundays, hoping in time to get the parents. This led to many congregations having fleets of used school buses, lots of underprivileged kids in Sunday School and lots of preachers going around to other churches telling them how successful the bus program was.

And you had the prison ministries. One year a church in Texas baptized about 600 people, over 400 of them prisoners. But I've never heard of many of those guys staying faithful on the outside.

We had Bible Chair campus ministries which taught college-level and -credited Bible courses on state college campuses. These ministries were like a Baptist Student Union, designed mostly for kids who grew up in the Church of Christ and now elected to go to a state school instead of an expensive Christian college. And the Christian colleges, Church of Christ private schools which were our version of seminary combined with a date and mate philosophy, were ninety-nine percent Church of Christ kids and pre-dominantly white. Except for the basketball teams which allowed 'em to be both integrated and evange-listic at the same time, since the highest concentra-tion of non-Church of Christ kids on the campus were darker-pigmented students who could dunk.

By the end of the sixties, the Churches of Christ had gone from being fast growing to simply struggling to keep their kids coming to church.

Then a campus minister named Chuck Lucas, in a Florida church called Crossroads, goosed the whole Church of Christ brotherhood in the early seventies by getting "heathen" college students from "secular" campuses to come to church in droves. This, all in the days before we had a MODERN DAY MOVEMENT OF GOD. It was just the Church of Christ...a bunch of nondenominational, autonomous, oft loving, always bickering hodgepodge of congregations spread across the country but most numerous in the Bible belt. Our current worldwide fellowship, now known as the "In-ternational Churches of Christ," has many of its roots in a melting pot of ministries, primarily a mixture of the most evangelistic ministries that existed in the Churches of Christ in the seventies.

When Kip went to Boston in 1979 and was suc-cessful in baptizing hundreds of kids from some of

*Sam Powell was converted in North Carolina and eventually became an evangelist and then an elder in the New York City church.*

the most elite campuses in the world, men and women from all across America began trekking to Boston for workshops and seminars. Many of them ended up moving to "be trained for the ministry" in Boston. This swung the influence of the campus ministries away from Crossroads, where Kip was converted, and toward the Boston church, which was perhaps the first congregation in which the adults agreed to fully support the ideology involved in building a totally committed congregation. Consequently, the singles and marrieds ministries in Boston were active from day one of the campus onslaught. Soul Talks were the basic organizational structure of the church. And I've always believed that the difference between Boston and other efforts in the sixties through the seventies in the Churches of Christ was the unity. The church elders were behind Kip and would not air any grievances in public. Hours were spent together becoming friends, ironing out differences and working together. All the members eventually understood and agreed that we were going to be different. If you were going to come to this church, you were going to try to be a "24/7" Christian. We studied the Bible and a skinny little book by Robert Coleman called *The Master Plan of Evangelism*. Heavy emphasis on the Bible and the Bible alone. But I shouldn't fail to mention Coleman's book. It was real popular among evangelicals of a certain ilk in the seventies, and we cut our teeth on the notions of imitating Jesus' vision and leadership style, primarily summed up by saying the book taught us to be focused on a few and duplicate ourselves...teach others who would teach others.

When we started in Boston in 1979, Kip and all the nuts like me who moved to Boston to be trained by him, we were still considered part of the Church of Christ fellowship. Different as we were, the Churches of Christ had been a contentious, debate-driven culture for nearly a hundred years, and we were tolerated for a while as renegades. Remember, this predated Macs and PCs. These were the days of telephones and mailing letters. Remember stamps? Faxes weren't even on the scene for the common man and shoot, CDs weren't even common in banking terms, much less musical. Communication between the congregations was mainly gossip, either in the form of newsletters and brotherhood magazines or just the regular old grapevine.

The three main brotherhood papers were the *Gospel Advocate* out of Nashville, *The Christian Chronicle* of Oklahoma, and *Firm Foundation*, edited by an elderly guru named Reuel Lemmons. In the late seventies if you were in a church with campus ministries that used Soul Talks as an outreach, then you were known as a "Crossroader." As more churches embraced that style of ministry, without even having a Crossroads trained minister in their midst, a more descriptive name evolved. The term Total Commitment Ministry became common in identifying a vast number of soul-saving churches, all allegedly in league with Chuck Lucas of Crossroads fame.

In *The Gospel Advocate* sometime around 1978, the term Total Commitment Evangelistic Movement was used to brand young ministers like me, working then for a church in Chattanooga, as a dangerous bunch of heretical loonies bent on false teaching. The guard was changing and the generation gap wasn't bridged peacefully. Then things got worse.

Kip's success in Boston dominated the ministry scene among evangelistic Churches of Christ and the stalwarts of the Churches of Christ old guard began talking about the Total Commitment Evangelistic Boston Ministries...I ain't kiddin'—you can't make this stuff up...and the lines began to get more clearly divided between already contentious churches.

In the mid-eighties Chuck Lucas, facing some personal problems, was dismissed by the Crossroads church. A lot of Crossroads people had been migrating to Boston for six years already, but with Chuck out of the picture, what had been assumed for a while became stated fact: Kip was the paramount leader of an evangelistic assault becoming more and more unacceptable to old guard Church of Christ people. The term "Boston Movement" was coined. But that term's main rival, thanks to Jim Jones and various Church of Christ periodicals, was the word "cult." Kip and other guys, mainly me, were asked less and less to visit other Churches of Christ and their workshops, seminars and such. Kip, who had been the most ovated and oft-invited speaker to a relatively famous Oklahoma workshop stopped getting invitations. Kip continued for a while to invite various personalities to speak in Boston, but as they became more and more vocal against what we were doing, it became easier to stop sending as many Christmas cards each year. We went from being the evangelistic celebrities of the Churches of Christ to the black sheep to personae non gratae. And to be honest, we were too busy to care a heck of a lot. We'd been preaching till we were blue in the face. And we were real young. And some of the men who had been my heroes growing up became vehemently opposed to us and made emotionally charged statements that simply weren't true. In time we got used to being the Boston Movement, the Soul Talkers, or the Totally Committed Evangelistic Boston Movement Dudes. But those who misunderstood us got more and more comfortable calling us a cult.

The adults in Boston weren't comfortable with the name Soul Talk for our small group Bible studies. They couldn't get past the Soul Train sound of it, and some folks felt like it wasn't being up front with people about what we wanted them to come to. So Kip started calling the studies "Bible Talks."

One of Kip's most brilliant moves, and a defining shift in our relationship with the Churches of Christ, was the decision to plant churches. Up until then, the way to spread the gospel was to train a campus minister and send him into an existing church. You then had a young, fired-up minister with a totally different agenda inside an older church, usually with lots of older members suspicious of the whippersnapper. Kip decided that we would just go ahead and plant new congregations. We were doomed to dividing existing churches if we didn't do something different, and doggone it, we were going to train missionaries and send them somewhere. Church planting began, and that more than anything led us to ultimately be known as a separate fellowship, the "International Churches of Christ," a preferred label over "cult."

That's an incredibly abbreviated, one-sided view of the first nine years of our fellowship's history. But I wanted to start there so I could tell you a little about the background of both us and what we now refer to as the "Mainline" or mainstream Churches of Christ.

We come from one of the most interesting stories in church history. In the late eighteenth century a large number of denominational preachers began to expound on what were then rather novel notions: Why do so many denominations exist? Are we not all brethren? Speak where the Bible speaks; be silent where the Bible is silent. No creed but the Bible; no name but Christian.

At the same time, a discovery of baptism as a crucial ingredient in man's acceptance of Christ began to unite these preachers. These were Presbyterian and Methodist men mostly, the leading personality being a Scottish family named Campbell, so that ultimately the Churches of Christ in later times would be called Campbellites by some folks, especially Baptists in a bad mood.

By the early sixties of this century, the Churches of Christ were recognized by an encyclopedia as the fastest growing church in the world and boasted over two million members worldwide. That's the church I grew up in.

My mother's father, his given names being John Wesley after you know who, would walk for miles to any tent meeting or church he could find. This ultimately led the young Methodist man to a Church of Christ meeting where he was baptized and began taking his brood of seven girls and four boys. But when my mom married my dad, he wasn't much of anything until it came time to go to church. Then he became a devout Baptist for a coupla' hours. To keep peace she went with him.

When I was five, a man named Doyle Key returned from Switzerland where he'd been a missionary. How he ended up in Clarendon, Arkansas, population 2,200, during cotton picking time, I'll never know. But after a lot of yelling and fussing in the bedroom, my mom got my dad to go see this man. And I still remember a night in 1959 when my dad came home with his hair still wet, and momma told me he got baptized. I had never seen a baptism, and when she described it to me, even at that young age, I realized that no matter how much my dad had resisted, this Doyle Key guy was able to hold him under the water. The yelling in the bedroom stopped, and we started going to the Church of Christ.

But by the end of the sixties what had been touted as the fastest growing church began to stagnate. Young people were leaving it by droves. But then young people were leaving all the churches in the sixties in droves.

The campus ministry movement was the most unlikely place for revival.

Chuck Lucas was the campus minister for the 14th Street Church of Christ in Gainesville, Florida, which is where the university is, of course. His incredible determination and charisma with young people would ultimately lead to three things: hundreds of college kids getting baptized, including Kip McKean; the building of a new church building so that 14th Street Church became the cooler-sounding Crossroads Church of Christ; and controversy.

A
♦

By the time I was eleven, I knew I was going to be a preacher. That was 1966. We lived in the middle of a soybean field halfway between Memphis and Little Rock. I went to Shiloh Church of Christ with my family. The name of our little community, Rural Route 1 out of Clarendon, was...Bethlehem. No joke.

October of 1967, a month before I turned twelve, I got baptized in a baptistery in a church in Brinkley, Arkansas, and the next year we moved to the Illinois side of the Mississippi in the St. Louis area. Only in his mid-thirties, my dad became an elder for the Church of Christ we attended in Granite City, and when I was fourteen, I met the guy who would cement my decision to become a preacher. He was my youth minister. His name was Terry Bell, and he was an older man who proved that you could be a Christian and be tough and cool and godly all at the same time. This guy was experienced, single, handsome, just returning from doing summer mission work in India, had his own rock and roll band and was...eighteen years old. Wow! I wanted to be just like Terry.

And let me tell you, that was a good thing to want to be.

The next summer we began with four teenagers active in our congregation. By September, after a summer of pizzas, bands, bonfires with Terry talking about how "twelve ragged men turned the world upside-down," and all night prayer sessions...we had grown to more than sixty teens in church.

Now, when Terry left, most of the kids did, too. They'd been summertime Christians.

But not me.

The deal was done. I wanted to follow Jesus like Terry.

I went to college. A Christian college. It was 1973, and that September life-changing things would happen to me. My favorite cousin died from an overdose of heroin the same day Jim Croce died in a plane crash. My grandmother died. And I flunked Greek because I'd gone off to school and instead of studying, I'd majored in Kathy Dixon.

But the sophomoric love pangs of a freshman Bible major really helped to set me up to meet the next role model in my life, Bob Brown.

Bob Brown was a John Wayne/Indiana Jones-like missionary in Trinidad. He was looking for students to come and work for him in the islands, and I didn't even know where the West Indies were. Something to do with Columbus, I thought.

But I got the gig. I went to the Caribbean for almost a year, and it's only thanks to God that I ever came back. Being with Bob remains, to this day, one of the greatest experiences of my life and taught me that there's a whole world out there that needs the gospel, and he was having a blast taking it to 'em.

When I finally did come back to the States, after a year again at my old school, I decided, mostly for economic reasons, to go back to Illinois to go to school. I had a state scholarship if I'd go to an Illinois school, and that, coupled with the good ole BEOG (who remembers those?), I'd be better off financially. And I prided myself in being self-supporting. That eased my conscience when my dad bailed me out with dough, as he would regularly.

Now, I say that the reason I went back to Illinois was financial. Truth is, I'm just lucky. (Remember, that means "blessed" in my vocabulary.)

It's August and I still haven't enrolled in college. Shoot, I haven't even picked a school yet, and I'm having a good time hanging out with this streaked-haired blonde I brought home to meet my folks. Wanna know how I met her?

I'll tell you anyway.

It's my last semester down south at Freed-Hardeman College, and I'm in this children's theatre group called the Pied Pipers, led by Uncle Hank McDaniel, my third mentor, first guru, in life. We'd do kids' shows on campus every other Saturday morning. We used no props and no real costumes, though we did have to wear "Piper Suits," which were these baggy jumpsuits that, in those days, only girls would wear in real life, under which I had to wear a flowing, blue blouse.

The day before Easter, 1976. I'm with my buddy just after a show. Still wearing our blouses, we go to the only pizza place in town which is run by a pal of mine. I walk in and...whoa...there sits on a stool at the bar, beside a girl I knew named Karen, this babe wearing a halter top with a tan dark as molasses. I hadn't seen that much flesh in public ever in Henderson, Tennessee, and without missing a stride, I cruise on in saying, "Karen, who's your friend? Why haven't you introduced me already? Don't you think she'll like me?"

"It's my last semester down south at Freed-Hardeman College, and I'm in this children's theatre group called the Pied Pipers, led by Uncle Hank McDaniel [shown here], my third mentor, first guru, in life."

Karen hangs her head and says, "Uh-oh, it's Johnson."

I keep walking toward them, drag my thumb across the babe's bare back and go behind the bar to pour myself a tall one. Well, a cold one. Coke that is. I've always been straight in that department.

Drink in hand, I come back around the bar and sit between Karen and the chick.

"Are you an airhead like Karen?" I ask, staring straight into these huge brown eyes.

"No, but you'll wish I was," she shot back, not flinching.

Nothing else much was said. They left. Fled. I shrugged and ate the pizza they had left. Hey, free food in those days....

The next day, Easter Sunday. My roommate, Ray, and I go to church. We always went to church. Only in this part of the world, there were thirty-six different Church of Christ congregations to choose from. Students were divided into groups of those who went to the same church all school year, or those who didn't attend regularly anywhere, or like me, those who never missed a service, but seldom went to the same congregation two weeks in a row for fear of actually getting involved. So on that Sunday, with thirty-six

*"I find out that her name is Lisa....We've been together ever since. Easter. 1976."*

choices, Ray and I go to Easter service, and sitting right in front of us are Karen and her friend.

After church they turn around, and Karen's friend says, "I like your suit better today."

She still hasn't let up. I find out that her name is Lisa. They leave.

I ask Ray if he'd like to ask 'em to lunch.

"If you ask 'em, I'll cook."

Ray was a darn good hamburger cooker. So, I run out in the gravel parking lot, and looking straight at Lisa, eyes locked, I say, "Karen, Ray says he'll cook if you two will have lunch with us."

And without another word spoken, Lisa looks straight at me and says, "I thought so."

We've been together ever since. Easter. 1976.

# A
♠

And in August of '76, still not knowing where I'd go to school, I take Lisa and a car full of teens to a statewide youth rally in Illinois. I'm one of the speakers. I'd grown up speaking at youth rallies all over the state, and it's at this event that God moved in another mysterious way.

Roger Lamb was the preacher for a little congregation called the Heritage Chapel Church of Christ. They had this picture-perfect church building, steeple and all, sitting in prime campus ministry retail space. Location, location, location. This building was on the edge of the campus, shouting distance from there to the high-rise dorms, and Roger had been the preacher there for a little while.

Lots of Churches of Christ in the north, or more exactly, outside the Bible belt, were considered missions. And they had little money. Roger had support from a church in Texas that helped pay his salary, and from time to time he'd have to report back to them on how things were going.

Roger took a group of kids to that same youth rally I was attending with Lisa and the gang, and I met him there for the first time. It turns out that he and my dad, both being Illinois Church of Christ preachers, had taken a road trip to a preacher's retreat together. They'd told jokes for hours in the car and had laughed enough to become friends. When Roger met me, the first thing he asked was where I was going to school in September. I told him I hadn't decided, and he told me I ought to come to Eastern; he wanted to start a campus ministry, and I'd be great to have there.

First thing, I'd never heard of Eastern Illinois University. It was tucked away inside a little town called Charleston which was surrounded by corn fields near the Indiana border. The population was 10,000 students, and the administration building looked like a medieval castle.

Second thing, I thought Roger was offering me a job. Besides being conceited, naive and slow on the uptake, I was always getting offers for jobs with little churches in Illinois and Missouri. When I was sixteen and a senior in high school, just before my seventeenth birthday, I landed a full-time, pulpit-preaching job for a little church in House Springs, Missouri. I went there three or four times a week, weekends and after school. Other kids were on sports teams, clubs, dates...I was a full-time preacher for a congregation of about twenty-eight adults.

It was an hour and a half drive in my '62 Healy, and after I graduated I moved into the parsonage for the summer before I went off to college. Parsonage? We never called 'em parsonages. They were the just the "preacher's house." Parsonages were something the Baptists had. The summer before I'd gone off to Freed-Hardeman College, I lived alone in a three-bedroom house next to the church building in House Springs, and the congregation had grown to nearly 100 on Sundays the year I preached there.

So, thinking Roger was asking *me* to be the campus minister wasn't that weird. Even though it was just a few weeks before school was going to start.

I was mulling his offer over in my head when he started talking about some guy named Kip McKean from Crossroads. I was well versed in all the old controversies in the Churches of Christ, but I'd never heard of Kip or Crossroads.

I never let on to Roger that I thought he was making a pitch to me to come be the campus minister. I was as proud as I was naive.

Roger filled me in and urged me to come to Eastern. Since no one else had given me good reasons to go anywhere else, and since Roger seemed to want me so bad, even if it was just to be a student, I got an application for Eastern and applied—it never occurred to me that I had to be accepted. I mean, who wouldn't want me? In a coupla' days, sure enough, they sent me a letter welcoming me to school. About the next day or so, I went to Charleston, without any housing arrangements, pulled my '68 six-banger, sky-blue Mustang into Roger and Marsha's driveway and stayed at their house until I found an apartment.

You could say that's how I became a World Sector Leader. I didn't have anywhere else to go.

I actually got to Eastern a day before Kip arrived. I heard he was in his office at the church building. September 1976. Steve Johnson meets Kip McKean. Two dudes who have no idea they're going to be friends for the rest of their lives. Me sure not thinking I'm about to meet my next mentor. Heck, he's only two years older than me, and he hadn't even been a Christian for more than four or five years. He was a Methodist, for goodness sakes, while I was preaching in Missouri. And he'd bombed out of his first campus ministry job in Philadelphia. How could I have dreamed he'd save my life and my soul?

And what could he have thought? I come into his office, unannounced, no knocking...a force of nature I am...twenty years old, one-week beard, overalls and barefoot. Not quite a hippie and not quite Ivy League either, I burst into a place I've been comfortable with my whole life: a preacher's study.

"Hey, you must be Kip! Great to meet you!"

He slowly stands, sticks out his hand to meet mine, and right off, I can tell this is different. I was accustomed to preachers falling all over me like a used car salesman on the last Friday of the month. After all, not many churches could get young men coming to church cause they *wanted* to be there, and usually preachers just went all out to be sure I didn't get away. Especially if they'd heard of me, and most of them in Illinois in those days had heard of me. But here was a guy not much more than my age, and what was he doing? Took me a few years of maturity later to realize in retrospect that Kip was "sizing me up." I'd never been sized up before.

"Yeah, I'm Kip. And you are...?"

"Steve. Steve Johnson. That your girlfriend?" I'd picked up a picture of this beautiful black-haired chick admiringly, and just as quickly, Kip took it out of my hands and set it back down where it had been.

"Yeah, that's my fiancée."

I felt a chill, and it wasn't 'cause I was barefoot on a hot day in early September.

That's how I first met the kid who'd become the leader of the MDMOG or the ICOC or, as I like to call it, "our fellowship." And that's the first time I saw Elena. In a pretty picture frame on a table by a desk in the office of a soon-to-be husband in a little town that would become the home of the baptizingest campus ministry in America.

Things didn't get much better for Kip and me that year. I look back and now understand how hard he was trying to pull me in. When he would go out of town, he'd have me lead the Bible Talks that first semester, fall of '76. Early in the game, he had me and two other guys speak on a Sunday night, and I batted clean-up, because of my experience I guess. So, he tried to reach out to me.

He'd come over to my apartment for what, in those days, we called "prayer partner" times. We'd eat bologna sandwiches covered with lettuce, mayonnaise and peanut butter. Kip taught me that peanut butter held everything together on your bread, and then we'd pray. But I never let him get in. And he had to be careful of me, I guess. He'd been burned badly in Philly, and he didn't want me to go nuts.

And I was courting Lisa.

She went to school that fall at my old alma mater, but every weekend, nearly, in September, October, November and December, she'd drive up to Eastern—an eight hour drive from Henderson, Tennessee. Or I'd go down to see her.

Imagine trying to work with a kid who's gone every weekend or with his girlfriend all the time?

Well, in December Kip got married, and I talked Lisa into changing schools and moving up to Illinois. She loved the ministry there more than I did, more than I could appreciate. For me it was just a new and weirder version of what I'd done my whole life. But for Lisa it was more.

That past Easter when I met the girl who would become my wife, she had just broken up with a boyfriend of four years. She was only eighteen and I was a wizened twenty, but she'd been going out with this guy since she was fourteen. He was older than she was, and they did drugs. Lots of drugs. Pot everyday. PCP (angel dust) was big back then. Ludes.

One day she walks into Leonard's Bar, their hangout, and has a moment of clarity.

Lisa's grandpa was an elder in the Church of Christ and a good guy. He'd quit a job during the Depression because they tried to make him work on Sundays. He had twelve mouths to feed, and he just walked out, went to church and trusted God to find him another job. Lisa grew up going to church with her family. But in her teen years she messed up. Until that day at Leonard's.

She went over to her boyfriend and said, "I'm getting out."

He didn't know exactly what she meant. But two days later she had a nut in a blouse and a colorful jumpsuit sitting between her and a friend asking, "Are you an airhead like...."

After Lisa and I met, she went back to Chattanooga and started going to church with a cousin who'd just returned from Sunset School of Preaching. This was one of those other places where things were happening in the Churches of Christ. Guys would move to places like West Monroe, Louisiana, to study the Bible and preaching and often become missionaries, as well as returning to the churches that had likely as not supported them to go to the school in the first place. Ken Erb, Lisa's cousin by marriage, studied with Lisa and baptized her shortly after we met. Lisa had found what she'd been looking for.

So, when she comes up to visit me on the weekends at Eastern, she gets excited. She loves Kip's devotionals, Roger's sermons, and what she sees with all the baptisms they were having is what she wants to do with her life. Me? I'm just figuring out that I want to do whatever she wants to do.

She moves to Charleston, and I give her my apartment. I move into my '68 Mustang and get a job at a deli. Now, I don't mind telling you about my sins and all the other stuff I did in the fall, winter and spring of '76-77, but it would bore most of you, and it's all been repented of. Suffice it to say that Lisa and I spent a lot of unaccounted-for time, and if it hadn't been for me, she would have been a good disciple and become Elena's best friend two years earlier.

But I pulled Lisa down. And her mother and dad started divorce proceedings. So, every other weekend we were driving from Charleston, Illinois, to Chattanooga. To be with her mom. And to get away from Kip.

Day after Valentine's Day, 1977. Lisa is working for Roger in his office. Out of pity, Roger gave Lisa a job typing. Lisa can't type. I go in to see Lisa and Roger says, "Steve, can I talk with you?"

Now there's a way a guy says "Can we talk?" and it doesn't mean much. Then there's the way Roger said it that day, so I know this is heavy, and Roger has always been nice to me. Kip's the bad cop; Roger's the good cop.

We walk back to the cry room.

The cry room is a nursery built in most Church of Christ buildings of that vintage. The nursery is a room in the back of the auditorium with a plate glass window so that the people with infants can see the service and a loud speaker on the wall so that they can hear the sermon. Poetic justice would mandate that the first heart-to-heart spiritual talk in which I'd listen to what was being said to me should occur in a cry room.

And you know...I don't remember everything Roger said. It's just that he took me aside to talk to me. He knew I was messing up with Lisa. But the better part of his speech was about how impossible it was for me to make a difference when I was gone all the time. My contribution to the talk centered on how I didn't want to be critical of Kip, but how I thought he was strange. I knew that what he was teaching and doing was Biblically sound, but I thought it was just another way to do what we'd been doing in the church for years, and I didn't particularly like Kip's flavor. With many other words Roger pleaded with me...but it was the guilt of my immorality that I silently focused on while he was talking.

After we finished, I went straight to Lisa and asked her to take a ride with me in the old Mustang. Snow was on the ground, and I cruised out to an old field, parked the car and told her we were going to get married.

"Really? When is this supposed to happen?" she laughed.

"Sometime before we die." Ever the vague one when it came to commitment, I thought I was safe.

"Sure. Well, it's not going to happen."

I can't pass up a chance to be dramatic when it's presented to me so sarcastically.

"Yes it will. Before this year is over."

Like Sarah, Lisa laughed. "No way."

Nine and a half months later, in December, we were married. I'm usually right about those kinds of things.

Between the day after Valentine's Day and our wedding, I changed a bit. Lisa and I left Charleston as soon as the semester was over. I had another serious talk with Roger, this one being about giving a good report on the ministry in Charleston to other preachers in Illinois, especially my dad. Roger was concerned that since I was leaving with unresolved issues in my life, I might have bad attitudes that I'd spread to anyone who'd listen. Roger was my friend and was sensitive, wise, in how he handled this. As for me, I knew that what Kip was doing was right. I just didn't think that was the way I wanted to do it.

Over the summer we set our wedding date and decided to be missionaries in Venezuela. Bob Brown recruited me again, and I spent a month and a half in Caracas while Lisa planned our wedding. When I came back to Chattanooga, I was offered a coupla' jobs. Lisa had already been appointed a full-time women's counselor for the campus ministry at the University of Tennessee in Chattanooga by Calvin Conn, the campus minister and occupier of the Church of Christ's Bible Chair at UTC. Calvin was fond of Crossroads and enamored of Kip and wanted someone who'd been a part of those ministries to assist him. Lisa got the job and shocked Kip at a seminar Chuck Lucas hosted the month I was in South America. When Kip saw Lisa at the conference, he was exceedingly kind and encouraging, and when I started working with Calvin, I found myself teaching and preaching things I heard Kip say for two semesters. By the time Lisa and I were married in December, I was a campus minister with Calvin, a youth minister at the next-door church, and Lisa and I were the house parents, complete with free apartment in the building owned by the Bible Chair, which was our student center. And I'd come to the realization that what Kip was doing wasn't alternative Christianity. It was discipleship, the real thing.

I called him and apologized. I told him that I'd thought we just had a personality conflict. What I really had was a sin conflict. I never wanted to open up

*Calvin Conn, a father in the faith. He was suffering with a migraine when I took this picture in 1978.*

about my life so we never got close enough to resolve issues. He was so moved by me calling that he arranged to pass by Chattanooga to see me during a trip he was taking with Roger. We went up to Lookout Mountain and prayed together and have been friends ever since.

We'd baptized about thirty people in the little church we'd been working with. Calvin thought that was great, and indeed, it was more than that congregation had done in years. And we were the only integrated Church of Christ, to boot. Still, I felt like it was pitiful compared to what was going on at that college in the corn field.

As we looked out over the lights of Chattanooga from a Civil War memorial, Kip told me this: "At least you're trying. That's something. Don't get discouraged, and don't feel like it's not much. You're trying, and the Lord must be pleased with that."

Over the next year or so, I'd call Kip from time to time, and when Lisa and I got really frustrated with our ministry, I set up an appointment with Kip to talk about our future.

In those days, most campus ministries either were ineffectual or ended up splitting their host congregations. There are lots of reasons why. Younger disciples were insensitive to older people who'd been coming to church forever. Emotional issues and monetary issues factor in, too. But Jesus said that you can't put new wine into old wineskins. I thought the new wine of youth and baptisms would rupture the old wineskins, and Lisa and I saw that beginning in our congregation.

We weren't united with our elders. We were united with Calvin, but he was often as frustrated as we were. Calvin always wanted to see the Church of Christ embrace the dynamic growth of the evangelistic campus ministries. And at Ole Miss, where he'd first served in the ministry, Calvin had stood up for integration even when opposition was thick in the Old South Churches of Christ. But now he knew that Lisa was crying every day because of the attitudes we were facing with the elders of our congregation, as well as the negative criticism we were getting from other Churches of Christ in the Chattanooga area. In fact the church where we were married, the Church of Christ where most of Lisa's family still attended and our friend and cousin Ken worked, this congregation had a minister who was calling all the other ministers in town to black-ball us and our campus ministry. They didn't like the term "Soul Talk," which is what we were still calling our small group Bible discussions, and so they began the humorous rumor that Lisa's Soul Talks were really seances and that one time she'd raised a cat from the dead. I laughed my head off at that one, but it would just make Lisa cry. These were men she had known or known of just about her whole life, and it hurt her that they were trying to harm us. To me, these were just another bunch of petty, small-town preachers afraid that Calvin's church was gonna get bigger than theirs. And I hated cats. No way would I'd have let my wife bring one back from the dead once it got what it deserved.

By this time we had successfully built a church-within-a-church at one of the congregations in Chattanooga. We were integrated, we were slowly baptizing, we were happy...as a group. But I knew, and Lisa knew even better than I did, that we were not going to be able to do much more. We'd done all we knew how to do, and we were on the way to splitting this church between the ones in our group who were growing and doing something and those who were just polishing pews with their backsides twice a week.

Lisa and I had abandoned dreams of going to Venezuela in order to stay and work with Calvin. I finally finished my undergraduate degree and began a graduate program in clinical psychology. "Began" is a bit grandiose. I was accepted into the graduate program, enrolled, and classes were about to begin when we moved to Boston. Here's how that happened.

Every year we'd go to the seminar hosted by Kip up in Illinois. His ministry had become the fastest growing campus ministry in America, with over 300 students baptized in less than two years on that tiny campus in the corn field. And now Lisa was crying every night, saying that we had to do something. We were over our heads. I'd preached my whole life, but I'd never led and organized a ministry even the size of our little one. I called Kip to see if he could give me some time to talk with him after the seminar, the one we took a Chattanooga group of twenty to attend in March of 1979.

Sunday after the service, there in that icon-like church building in Charleston, Kip took me back into the same little office I'd bounced into barefoot nearly three years earlier. I told him I'd done as much as I knew to do and that I was thinking of taking a sabbatical to train for the ministry. Where did he think I should go? I liked the guy in Denver, Tom Brown; he was cool. I could go there. Or should I go to Crossroads? What do you think, Kip?

He paused and said that if he took this job he was being offered in Lexington, Massachusetts, that Lisa and I ought to come up there with him and Elena.

I was stunned. For two reasons.

For one thing, in those days, having a successful

campus ministry like Kip did in Charleston was rare. Shoot, it was nearly unheard of, and Kip's was hands down the best there was then, and even better for him being the minister to make it happen in a small place where they started off by calling him Jim Jones. No one, certainly not me, would have dreamed that Kip would consider leaving Charleston. This was his pride and glory.

Second, I never would have thought that he'd want me to go with him anywhere. I would've expected him to say, "You want to go get trained? Good! You need it. Go to Florida, go to Denver, just do me a favor and STAY AWAY FROM BOSTON!"

But he wanted me to consider coming with him. I was surprised and deeply moved.

Nothing was definite for him at that point. A family named the Gempels lived in Concord and were part of the tiny Lexington Church of Christ, a congregation that was about to close its doors and merge with the Burlington Church of Christ. The Gempel's son, Doug, went to Duke and fell in with a bunch of campus ministry renegades with ties back to Crossroads, which gave them the impetus to call Chuck Lucas and begin talking about getting a campus minister for the Lexington church. Chuck knew Kip's dream was to go to Boston. Kip and the Lexington group got in touch, and eventually, the deal came down to the Lexington elders and the Gempels needing to see firsthand what was going on in Illinois before Kip would even consider the job. He'd had his bad experience in Philly, and now the church that had supported Roger for years, that Texas church, had stopped their support because of the association with Crossroads. Funny how weird people can get about names like "Soul Talk" and such.

I went back to Chattanooga and told Calvin what Kip and I had talked about. Calvin was one of the coolest people to ever walk the earth. He'd busted his tail to get things together for us in Chattanooga, getting my salary; he'd gone to bat for me against the anti-raising-dead-cat preachers of Tennessee; and now I was telling him I'd like to go with Kip to Boston.

"I don't want you to go, Steve."

We were sitting in my '65 Mustang convertible, a car that Calvin had helped to talk down mean ole Mr. Bird at the used car place where I'd bought it. Heck, Calvin even helped me buy my car, and I was abandoning him.

"I don't want you to go, but I'll tell you...."

Calvin was great at pregnant pauses. One time in his office he was talking and rocking in his desk chair and midsentence rocked back too far and fell over with

*The Gempel family circa 1979: (left to right) Kim Arthur, Bob Gempel, Pat Gempel, and Doug Arthur*

his huge feet facing out where his mouth had just been, and after a pause...kept right on talking. Only missed one beat. One pregnant pause. Funny guy.

"...if Kip asked me to go, I'd go. I'd go if I were you, and it kills me to say it. I'd go just about anywhere Kip asked me to go."

Calvin had just turned forty and Kip was nearly twenty-five. I respected Calvin like no one else at that time in my life. It'd be real arrogant to go on and on about how sacrificial Calvin was being, since the object of sacrifice was none other than me. But we'd worked hard to carve out a way to try to build something in Chattanooga that defied the rules Satan wanted us to abide by, and now I was talking about taking a powder. And Calvin was letting me go. Encouraging me to not miss the opportunity.

**A ♣**

Kip decided to move to Lexington, and on his birthday in May 1979, he drove his little gang out to Lexington and soon held the devotional in the Gempel's living room that would become the official start of the movement so many of us are now a part of. That same Friday night, I was starting two different Bible studies with a coupla' Baptist guys at UTC. That's right. I wasn't really one of the thirty would-be disciples on that fatefull night. I was about 850 miles south of there.

Kip and I had since talked, and I wasn't real sure what the Lord wanted. That's how us holy people talk when we're not sure we want to do something or not. "Don't know what the Lord wants me to do..." is how we stall. I was having a real hard time leaving Calvin and the group we had built. Lisa was ready to pack. We'd agreed to take a trip to visit Boston in July.

We went up to Boston and stayed with Kip and Elena for two weeks, and at the end of it Kip took us out fancy: a Friendly's down the road from him. There he gave us the hard sell. Lisa had already made her mind up and truth was, I had, too. I just got a kick out of making Kip want us so badly. Guess I hadn't changed that much after all.

And it was there in that Friendly's that Kip did one of his funniest Kipisms.

He was talking about how much we needed to come to Boston and how cool it would be—how I'd be the oldest guy he was training and you never know, I could end up his associate minister and stuff like that. Then he said, "And Lisa, we could get you to live in the dorms with the sisters there. And Steve, you could probably be in Cambridge with some of the guys...."

I knew that it would take a total commitment to move to Boston and be trained by this guy. And I knew he'd be radical and expect me to be, too. But he could tell by the looks on our faces that we were faltering.

"Well, I don't mean it would have to be the dorms and Cambridge. It could be anywhere. But you guys will set a great example in the households you'll be in. Is there anyone you'd like to live with?"

Then it dawned on us: he forgot we were married.

"We'd kinda like to live together, if that'd be okay."

Funniest look in the world is Kip's when embarrassment sets in.

I told Kip I'd call him in a coupla' days; I needed to pray more about it, didn't know what the Lord wanted me to do...and we started for Chattanooga, stopping in Manhattan on the way back, to see an old buddy of mine named Keith Watson.

Keith was the other guy in a Piper suit the day I met Lisa, and he was now a starving actor in New York. We spent a few days with him. He lived in a basement apartment on the upper west side. This meant his windows were sidewalk level. And he had no air-conditioning, which meant that in the heat of July all those windows would be open in the middle of the longest garbage strike in New York's history. Which meant right outside the opened basement windows were weeks and weeks of garbage piled up and ripe. For the next four years this would be what I thought they meant by "If you can make it there...."

I promised Lisa as we pulled onto the New Jersey Turnpike, world's ugliest road, that we might move to Boston, but I'd never move her to New York City. Yup, word for word that's what I said back in the summer of '79 driving south on I-95.

We returned home and I returned to my studies with the two Baptist guys. They didn't get baptized... but I did.

In studying with them, I became convinced that my baptism at age eleven was no more valid than theirs. They believed they had been saved before they got dunked, the baptism being an "outward expression of an inward feeling." I believed that I wasn't saved until after I got dunked, but as I studied repentance, discipleship and walking in the light, I realized that at that early age, I really didn't know what it was all about. I was smart enough at eleven to know that the Bible taught that you had to get baptized to have your sins washed away, and I felt guilty about enough stuff, even at that age, to worry every night when I prayed, "if I should die before I wake...."

But as I studied with these guys, I realized that the Bible clearly taught that repentance was a prerequisite for scriptural baptism, and I couldn't really remember if I knew what I was doing or not. I knew that at that age, my mother was taller than me. I couldn't really remember my little mother ever being taller than me, so I knew I could never put confidence in a decision I had made at that young age. I called Ken, Lisa's cousin, and said I needed to talk. He was my best friend and lived walking distance away. By now, we were packing a U-Haul truck to move to Boston. The next day we'd be driving to Lexington. It was August 29, 1979. I walked over to Ken's and told him I needed to get baptized.

Now you have to understand that these were like the Jurassic days of counting the cost. So many people ask me what was it like being in "The Movement" in the beginning. We didn't know we were in a movement. We were just a bunch of Christians trying to do what Jesus said to do in Matthew 28. When I told Ken I needed to be baptized, he counted the cost with me. That amounted to not much more than asking, "Are you sure?"

I told him why I questioned my dunking at age eleven. I told him I didn't just want to be sure. I wasn't just wanting to cover all the bases. I believed that I was lost and what convinced me the most was realizing that the one thing that stood in my way was pride, just like anyone else. The pride that makes someone feel like they just can't believe that all those years they thought they were saved they were really lost. The last obstacle for me was admitting that in spite of my preaching, early faith—everything that had mattered up till then—I was lost. The thing that helped the most? Realizing God had spared me to come to this decision and loved me so long to bring me to the realization that no one is good enough to be saved. We all have to trust and obey.

Ken and I, and Lisa, sneaked into the church building where Ken worked. He was on our side, but this was the very place that housed the pulpit that our biggest detractor preached from. Enemy territory.

It was also where our wedding took place.

Like burglars, we stole into the sanctuary, jumped in the baptistery which was right behind the podium where Lisa and I had pledged our love one-and-a-half years earlier. I told Ken, "Hold me under until I tap you on the wrist; I don't want to ever forget this one."

He did...and I haven't.

The next day we drove to Boston, and I've always believed that Kip was a little ticked off that I didn't wait till I got there to let him baptize me. But no way I was driving through New Jersey one more time with a lost soul.

So, there it is. We missed the devo with the thirty would-be's and got to Boston in the fall, three months after Kip got there. We had raised support so that we could train full-time for the ministry. Calvin had got some for us. Churches I had spoken for gave us some. I didn't know until just before Calvin died, but my father-in-law had given about $100 a month to him to send to us and didn't want us to know who it was from. Altogether, Lisa and I had an income of $700 a month.

We found an apartment in Cambridge for $400 a month and we dropped $50 a week in the plate passed at church. So, we were living on $100 a month for food and gas. We ate rice three times a day. I could turn this into a recipe book—all the things you can do with Spam, brown sugar and rice.

A few times we ran out of money and a check would come from nowhere. Once, when we left our apartment with bare cupboards, we came home to find $80 worth of groceries on the counter in our little kitchenette. And you know, those were glorious days.

No, I wasn't one of the would-be's, but nine months later, May of 1980, Kip made me the first evangelist he ever appointed in the Boston church. I was his Associate Evangelist. I got a raise. Heck, I finally got a salary. We ate rice a little less and ordered pizza to celebrate. And it was glorious.

I hope I'm not boring you. I just thought you might like to know some of this stuff. 'Cause, you see, this worldwide fellowship of ours, which, at the moment that I'm writing, consists of 360 congregations in 153 different countries, came from that little church in Lexington that in 1979 was home for a bunch of dreamy, young, missionary-hearted people who wanted nothing more than to spend all of our time studying the Bible with people and baptizing them. We didn't have pensions. Dang it, like I said, most of us didn't even have salaries. At least not at first and not for a long time.

Lisa and I were the only married couple training full-time with Kip and Elena. But there were a total of nine people who took the Acts class on Saturday mornings with Kip. Doug Arthur, Jim Lloyd, Tim Anderson,

Gordon Blasius, Fred Faller, Chris Timmons (now Fuqua), Lynne Hembree (now Greene), and Lisa and me—these are the ones I remember off the top of my head. Maybe there were a coupla' more, but not more than a couple. These were the people who Kip taught on Saturday and then sent out with these lessons to teach others.

Again, folks always ask, "What was it like to be trained by Kip back then?"

Let me say, first thing, Kip has always been inspiring.

But being trained by Kip, for me, was like this: We went door knocking one day, inviting people to Bible Talk. We knocked a few doors, Kip showed me how to do it, then sent me to do it some more.

We started a Bible Talk. Kip led one time, had me lead the next one, then never came back. You're on your own, dude.

I started a study with a guy in the Navy named Dave. I asked Kip what to do. We'd take the Saturday classes, and Kip would tell me to teach whatever he taught on Saturday. I did that and in four weeks baptized Dave. You could say that's how I became a world sector leader. I just kept baptizing Daves until there were a whole bunch of 'em.

And in the early days, I wasn't really one of the

boys. I was a married man and didn't always include myself in their late night talks and prayer sessions and video games and such. I was too busy to realize it at the time, but there was quite an aggravation on the part of some of the young guys, especially Doug Arthur, about the way I seemed to always agree with Kip.

Once, we had a talk about it, and I explained that I hadn't moved to Boston to question Kip, but to learn from him. I'd been married two years now and had preached darn nearly my whole life. I told Doug, and whoever else would listen to me, that I already knew what I knew. I'd moved my whole life to Boston to learn what Kip knew and had made myself a promise that unless Kip asked me to do something unscriptural, then whatever he said, that's what I'd do. I'd already failed in the ministry before. I doggone sure wasn't going to be a "failure." I came to learn and succeed.

I got a call from one of the guys late one night. He was upset and had decided to leave Boston. Kip had offended him. The brother had driven Kip to the airport for one of Kip's preaching trips and on the way Kip had made some strong suggestions about how the guy needed to change if he wanted to be in the ministry. This was a young, charismatic Southerner who didn't like what Kip had to say and just wanted me to know why he was leaving.

I drove over and brought the dude back to my house where we talked all night, until the sun came up, and we were still talking. I told him how I'd decided to come to Boston and how I already know what I know and you just heard the speech a paragraph or two ago. But then I had him read Philippians and Ephesians with me. This was one of my epiphanies in life, a defining moment that would steer me forever—and it came about as the result of reaching out to a young guy who wasn't sure how much he wanted to learn from a guy like Kip.

I said, "'Submission' has been a dirty word in our lifetimes. Say it and you think, 'doormat,' as in gettin' walked on. But Paul said in Ephesians 5:21 to submit to each other out of reverence for Christ. Submit. Not just wives to husbands, but brother to brother. And not because the person you submit to deserves it. In Philippians he says that we ought to consider others better than ourselves. Why?

"Why not? What does it hurt? Pride, yeah. That gets stomped on. Selfish ambition gets squashed—or at least put on hold for a while—when you consider others more important than yourself. But it's the only way you ever learn stuff you don't already know. And it's the only way you build unity.

"I already have led a ministry, but I haven't

baptized 300 people in the middle of nowhere like Kip did. And I have no chance of doing that if I don't learn what he knows. Do what he does. That's why I'm here. And I've decided to trust him. What's it gonna hurt?

"Now I believe in the Lord and I believe Kip. I think he wants to save the lost. We're different. But if I could push a button and become just like him, warts and all, then, well...for the sake of the cross, I'd push that button, because I don't think there's anyone alive who wants to save souls more than Kip McKean. I'm gonna submit because that's what the Bible says to do to the least of my brothers, much less someone who's gonna help me turn the whole world upside-down."

The guy stayed in Boston and became an evangelist. And I began figuring out what my role in life was. If Kip was explosives, I was glue. Everything he did made sense to me, and I saw at least a part of my job being to help others, especially knuckleheads, to understand and hang in there.

The schedule we had back then was rigorous by today's standards, I think. But, you know, it was a blast!

We had two services on Sunday, for everyone. Sunday mornings we had a Bible class before the services. I taught the college students and Kip the adults. I loved it. Then we had Sunday morning services, and Kip always preached, except when he was out of town and then I usually was the speaker. Sunday evenings Kip spoke and while the morning service was more devoted to visitors, the evening was for the members. These services are legendary for us old-timers. Kip would get on a roll, and we'd hear the same points made week after week until Kip was satisfied we all got it. Every week he'd talk about the bitter root in Hebrews 12 and coming to all the services from Hebrews 10. Acts 2 was visited ALL the time. Drop your Bible and it would fall open to Acts 2. And Kipisms were imitated by the brothers, both seriously and humorously.

One Sunday night Kip was preaching on marriage and thundered, "MEN, LOVE YOUR HUSBANDS!"

"AMEnnnnn," the crowd followed for a second, then realized the false doctrine a moment before Kip blushed.

Another favorite was when he bellowed, "The humble shall be EXHAUSTED!!!"

"AMEN!"

I don't think half the crowd even realized that it was a slip of the tongue. It was too true a statement, whether Kip said "exhausted" or "exalted" like he'd intended.

We had Soul Talks in our first year, but we changed the name to Bible Talks. These were our small group

Bible studies. This is how we built the movement, trained leaders, baptized folk, moved the masses. All of us training or in the ministry led at least four or five Bible talks. Most members were in at least two, unless they had small children. I had Bible Talks on Monday, Tuesday and Thursday nights and eventually a coupla' daytime ones.

Wednesday nights were classes. Kip taught the Acts class to the whole church. We had memory verses, quizzes and tests on the studies we were to do with non-Christians, and then he'd go chapter by chapter through the book of Acts so that when we finished, no matter how short a time someone had been familiar with the Scriptures, "at least you knew one book of the Bible." He'd have you learn at least three things from each chapter so that the average member could go through the book by memory and tell you what had happened in each chapter. Our members knew more in three months than most seminary graduates ever know.

Then, every Friday night, the whole congregation had a devotional together. We had most of these the first year in Kip's parsonage basement. Until we were having over 130 people. By that time we had grown out of the Lexington church building and were renting the Arlington Baptist church and held devos there. I'll tell you more about the building sagas in a second.

These devos were varied. We'd have lessons, praying times, sharing. Always starting at exactly ten minutes after eight and always followed by fellowship and refreshments. These were the highlight of the week, and sometimes folks would be chased out at midnight.

Then on Saturday mornings we had our classes with Kip. Okay, maybe it's kissing up, but I gotta tell you, Kip is the best. No matter what we were feeling; tired, discouraged—he'd fire us up. Happy, cocky— he'd level us. Moved and instructed by the Scriptures and inspired by what God was doing, we developed a sense of destiny. We began to witness and understand that something special was happening in this little church.

For one thing, we weren't little much longer. At our bring-your-neighbor day that first fall, we had 176 people in attendance. The little Lexington church building, whose doors were going to be closed before Kip came there, was bulging with people. Folks who'd been there for a long time were crying. It was a dream come true.

The contribution began to grow. Thank God. That's how I got hired the following spring. We had the money to grow.

We had baptisms at every service. The first year Kip was there, 102 or -3 people got baptized. Like I said, I think Kip wished I'd got baptized in Lexington to make it 104.

And we began talking about buying a building. In time we settled on making a deal for a Baptist church on the historic registry located in the South End of Boston.

But another thing I gotta tell you. Some of the people who were there before left when Kip arrived. They didn't like the length of services—or the length of some of the people's hair. Some didn't want to quit smoking and some didn't want to go to "Soul Talks." One family felt like the building they'd built with their bare hands was being ripped away from them. Believe what you will, but Kip did everything he could to lose no one. He put me on the case of a number of older folks who I really cared about and tried to get to hang in there. But by Christmas of '79 it was clear that everyone who had stayed was wanting to work for the Lord. And anyone who wanted to leave had left. And we were growing out of the little Lexington building with each passing service.

Going into our second year, we had to find a bigger place to worship. As I recall, the Gempels and Kip and a few others formed a building committee and did two things: rented the Arlington Baptist church and started in earnest a search for property to buy. By the third year we had added the school next door to our Sunday rental situation and gone to two, simultaneous services. And we'd had a fire.

Our building search led us to a purchase agreement for a landmark building in Boston's South End. In the early eighties the South End hadn't gotten gentrified yet, and some saw our purchasing this building as a positive event in turning a run-down area around.

But Boston had lots of fires that year. Arson was rampant and the building we had put so much of our hopes into got torched. I don't remember who called me, but I was living in Cambridge then, and I got to the scene before Kip did. The local TV crews were there, and when they learned a minister for the church was present, they came and stuck a mic and camera in my face, not that I was shy at all, and asked me what we'd do.

"Well, this building represented so many of our hopes and dreams, for our congregation as well as for the community...blah, blah, blah...," went my first TV interview. I was sad and tried to project the senseless loss I felt the occasion deserved.

Kip walks up. The brothers gather around. Kip smiles, shrugs. "Well, we have to be glad this happened. It must've been too small. It wasn't God's will for us to have this building."

Another lesson from the boss. I'm seeing tragedy; he's seeing God's will.

And of course he was right. The building was way too small. We continued to have two services, and a year later I was in New York and the Boston church began meeting at the Boston Garden regularly. That was unbelievable! The old Lexington church building we started out in had been converted into church office space and a twenty-four-hour baptistery service station. But several years later, it would prove to be too small for even that, and the church sold it and held no property except the old parsonage. This would set a trend, and we'd end up with a philosophy of not owning property by default. Not that we had any doctrinal stance against the church owning a building. We just kept growing out of anything we could afford. Our baptisms made every place we met eventually become obsolete, at least until we started meeting in places like the Garden on a regular basis.

And at the end of that third year we sent out our first mission team. To London. Doug Arthur and Jim Lloyd and their wives, with four other people, planted a congregation in England. And this is as good a place as any to tell you that if Kip had been just another preacher wanting to have his own big church, the story of the last twenty years would be totally different. And

I gotta tell you, if it'd been up to me, he would've been the preacher for the biggest church in the history of America, and it would've been right there in Boston, and I would've been right beside him. But he's always had more vision than me, and if it weren't for Kip, Lord only knows what would've become of me.

I wanted to stay with Kip in Boston forever. Back in those days, everybody was trekking to Boston to find out what was going on, and most of the ones who visited...stayed. We were still considered part of the Churches of Christ, in spite of the fact that so many of the old guard preachers despised what we were all about. Kip and I would be invited all over the country to speak, and for a while it looked like we would carry the day. I mean, it looked to me like we were more popular than despised.

But in 1981 we were having our Ministry Training Program classes, the Saturday class which had evolved from that first Saturday Acts class with about nine of us into the basement of the Arlington Baptist church. Kip was mulling over in his head a plan he hadn't fully let me in on yet.

The class, now about sixty of us, did reports on universities around the world. It became a room full of maps of all the major cities in all the countries on Earth. We sat in a room surrounded by maps, and each team gave their report orally. And it all came together for me. What Kip wanted to do. And I realized we could do it. As impossible as world evangelism seems to one person, if each of us took a city and did what Kip had done in the last two and a half years in Boston, then we could do it. In one lifetime. I was getting as excited as a spectator watching the solution for Fermat's last theorem getting worked out on a chalkboard.

Kip had been talking about how the only way to send out trained ministers without splitting churches was just to start new churches. This may seem like the most obvious thing in the world today, but it was revolutionary back then. He immediately began working with Doug and Jim to get them ready for London, a dream they'd had for a while. A dream to spread the gospel and to get out of Boston and be on their own. And Marty Fuqua wanted to go to Chicago. Or maybe Kip wanted Marty to go to Chicago? At any rate, by 1982 the church in London was planted, as well as the church in Chicago and sixteen other target cities were announced in our Boston bulletin.

I don't remember exactly how it happened that the idea of Lisa and me leaving and planting a church came up. Probably was Lisa, who has always seen the bigger picture before I did. But I clearly remember that

I wanted to stay with Kip. But I wanted him to want me to stay. I did a stupid thing.

Kip and I always got together around 10:00 PM on Tuesdays. I'd drive over to his house or meet him at a HoJo's on Route 128. This one Tuesday night in the spring of '82, I drive over to his house and tell him I've been thinking about starting a church in L.A. or Manila or maybe Mexico City or even New York.

"Awesome! That's what I've been wanting to talk to you about. You'd be great starting a church somewhere!"

That was Kip's response.

Now, I wanted him to say that I'd do a great job but that he needed me, wanted me to stay with him, that Boston would fall apart without me, and he'd have no fun if I was gone. "Please stay, Steve," was what I was wanting to hear.

But I never told him that. When he responded that way, so joyous, fired-up and downright happy to see me go...my heart got senselessly broken. I didn't understand how important it was for the kingdom to expand; I just wanted to be Sundance to Kip's Butch. But that wasn't what he wanted. And I resolved to leave and start a congregation somewhere.

The somewhere soon became New York, the greatest city on Earth as far as I'm concerned, and the greatest move I ever made in my life. And Kip was wind in my sails. But it took a long time to come to grips with my feelings and come to terms with what my destiny was supposed to be.

The next few months became months of getting ready to leave. Lisa and I began trying to put together a team and soon had planned a devotional in Manhattan for the winter before we'd plant the church, the planting date being set for June of '83. I wanted that date because it was as close as I could get to starting when Kip had started, and I was determined to imitate as much as possible everything that Kip had done in Boston. I was determined not to fail, and I wanted his playbook. I'd run the same plays he did, and by golly, that way maybe I'd win the game.

In fact, when Kip asked me what I wanted for a going-away present, I told him there was only one thing: I wanted hardbound copies of all the Boston bulletins since we'd started in '79. They were the only written record kept, and if I was real serious about this book being accurate, I'd refer back to them to refresh my memory. But right now we're just sitting in my back yard yakking. But, if anyone ever wants to write a real, detailed account of what we did back then, memories, those bulletins and a few dog-eared pictures are all there is. I wanted those bulletins, because I was determined to follow step by step, week by week in Kip's efforts to follow Jesus' steps. And that's what I did.

Doug and I weren't friends then. We weren't enemies—heck, we were brothers. But I'd been aloof as an old married guy when he was just a whippersnapper college student, and he'd been very critical of Kip and ergo, me, 'cause he thought I was just a "yes man" for Kip. When I left for New York, Doug asked Kip, "Do you think he'll make it on his own?"

When I went to New York, to borrow a phrase from the Houston rocket man, "Failure was not an option." I was confident for three reasons: I knew God wanted us to succeed, I knew Kip was the best teacher I could've had, and Lisa had to go with me. I always figured that even if I didn't convert any men, Lisa would baptize women and where you got women, eventually you'd get men.

New York got a bad rap from the very beginning. People would say the women are awesome but the brothers are not "kick down the door" leader types.

When we came to NYC, we had a total of eighteen people on the team. Only four were men. Why? That's all I could get. Now in September (we'd started in June) Kip let the Taliaferros move to be with us. I'd recruited Mike to Boston in '82 and wanted him to go with me.

At first Boston wouldn't let go of him. Think contract.

I begged; think free-agency.

In the bottom of the ninth, we got him, but he had to finish up the summer in Salem and then come on down.

In 1983 the *New York Times* reported that the census said there was a seven to one ratio of females to males in New York City. Now, nearly sixteen years later, we have 2,600 men and 3,100 women in the congregation. I've always felt like we had some tough hombres in the church here; it's just that our women are so doggone awesome that a New York brother has to smoke dynamite and shave with a chain saw in order to appear half as rough as the rest of the wimps around the world.

When we started in 1983, women's counselors were all single women. They were really sort of like what we'd call interns today. If a woman was married and in the ministry, like Lisa, she was just "a preacher's wife."

When we started printing bulletins, which, by the way, were for the Central Park Church of Christ, our first incorporated name in the Big Apple, I told Lisa I had a surprise for her. When she looked at the bulletin, her name was on it as the women's counselor. She was happy. That was a good week.

Soon, all the churches in our fellowship were calling their preacher's wives "women's counselors" (later we switched to "women's ministry leaders") and eventually Kip would give Lisa and me credit for establishing the principle of all the churches being led by married couples. Whatever. I just always knew I was sunk without Lisa. God'd done some pretty amazing things to love me in my life. Great parents, great influences— but nothing greater than Kip for a teacher and Lisa for a best friend. Wife, yeah. But more. She's been my best friend for nearly twenty-four years.

# A

Is it just me or are you getting tired? I'm sorry, I didn't really intend to go on and on about this stuff. For the last few weeks I've been writing on the Internet and I'm getting in the habit of just writing like we were talking and had all day, but I know you're busy, and I really didn't mean to get into all this ancient history. And by the way, reason why we haven't got much of this stuff written down already is because my buddy Kip is a lot more interested in making history than writing about it.

But since I've come this far I'd better tell you two or three other things before I end this FIRST BOOK I EVER WROTE IN MY WHOLE DOGGONE LIFE.

Over the years, since '79, Kip and I have disagreed on more than we've agreed on, I'm sure. We've had fights, I've had 'TUDES, and we've argued and debated.

But we're still together. We've always resolved our issues, and we've always agreed on the things that mattered the most.

Kip never asked me if he could be my leader. I've just been running to keep up for twenty years. And he's been reaching out to me, covering up for me and hanging on to me for all that time. A better friend you could never have, and a wilder partnership could not exist.

I resolved to be united and not to be divisive and dogmatic on issues that might just change in a little while anyway. A little advice: the kingdom is like the weather in New England; if you don't like it, wait a minute, and it'll probably change.

Doug and I have become more like best friends. And that's all his fault, er, credit.

Jim Lloyd was Doug's best friend, and when things didn't work out for him to stay in London with Doug, Doug eventually called me. He'd realized that, whadd'ya know, Steve made it on his own down there in New York after all. When Doug looked around for a peer to become pals with, he saw none other than me.

He and I agreed on the phone to meet in Atlanta. He was speaking there, and I flew down, and we stayed up all night establishing what would become both an "iron sharpens iron" relationship and a "lots of laughs" friendship. I finally understood that I wasn't all that much older and more experienced than the Dougs or Frank Kims or Scott Greens, and Doug realized that I wasn't a bozo after all. At least that's what I finally conned him into believing.

Not long after that (about '87 or '88), Kip gathered a group of about twenty of us together to discuss how we'd stay united from that point on. We'd all gone out and tried to imitate Kip, including starting churches all over the world. Problem was, we all wanted to go to the same places, at least the same countries. We were racing to recruit team members, and competition was reaching divisive levels. And Kip had about fifty men scattered around the world who would listen to no one but him.

Our meeting was in the famous Gempel's living room. Kip, after much prayer, led the discussion which would be the talk that gave birth to what we now call "world sectors."

The consensus was simple enough: we all wanted Kip to lead, and we all wanted to be a part of evangelizing the world in our generation. I'd grown up hearing men preach about world evangelization. In the late seventies some of those same men had met in Texas and signed a statement admitting they'd failed in their time to accomplish the Great Commission. Darned if that was going to happen to us. We all agreed that Kip should take inventory of what we collectively had and follow the Lord's example: choose a few of us and divide up the chores left for us to turn the world upside down in our day. That's how we began talking about the world sectors. And that's what began to clearly define us as a movement, separate from the Churches of Christ as a whole.

To this day, we've never felt that world sector leaders are some Biblical office. We fully know that we invented it, and for what it's worth, when we're playing hearts or any time idle talk is rampant, we debate what will become of the role when we're dead and gone. We simply needed an organizational way to keep all the congregations united and use the resources we have to get the job of evangelizing this world done.

I'm not a scholar, but I can read as good as a Presbyterian. The unique thing about us in church history so far is that we've spread out around the world so much and still stayed together. Every church in our fellowship was either planted since '79 by someone tied back to the Boston church, or was a reconstruction—a "reconstruction" being one of the few existing congregations that asked us to come and help them so they could be a part of our fellowship, instead of us just starting a brand new congregation in their city from scratch.

In all of church history, groups have splintered by now. Johnsons have disagreed with McKeans who've fought with Arthurs and you'd have variations of denominations every time you turned around—or opened a hymnal.

We're still working together. And still friends and fans of each other. I believe that's why God has blessed us.

The Bible clearly teaches that only one way exists to be saved. But we only get to be part of that if we strictly adhere to Jesus' teachings. We could argue over words, as Paul told Timothy not to do, and we could tolerate false teachings, as John writes about the Lord condemning in Revelation, and end up missing the grace God has given us. But our strength has been in our love for the Bible and our loyalty to each other. And our willingness to let time help us figure out slippery issues.

We've been dumb sometimes, but smart others. It was smart putting in place a uniform administrative system of financial and legal policies for all of the congregations. We're going to get called a lot of negative things, so it's good that our members can know beyond a shadow of a doubt where the money's going and what our intentions are. I don't believe that preachers have ever been better taken care of and at the same time protected from accusations of greed like we are in our fellowship. We have lots of tireless administrators to thank for that, but none more than our World War II vet brother, Cecil Wooten. On the smart end, he's first-rate and should our history ever be of any real importance, he oughta be prodigiously famous.

We may not ever be able to really put a dent in the poverty, sickness and abandonment around the world today. But we're trying. The Gempels have gone from that famous living room to leading HOPE Worldwide, spending themselves selflessly in the efforts of doing good in the name of Jesus everywhere. While our labors with them may never be fully accomplished, one thing I have dedicated myself to, and I hope you'll join me: as we go about fulfilling our first and foremost mission directive, to seek and save the lost, there is no reason in the world why we can't take care of our own. We may not be able to adopt all the orphans, or house all the homeless or feed all the hungry in the world. We won't be able to start enough hospitals to heal all the sick and diseased or enough clinics to minister to all the lepers and HIV- and AIDS-infected souls. But we can create and establish a family of believers who love each other enough, are sacrificial, so as to see to it that none of our members anywhere need ever go without a roof over their head, a meal in their stomach, a family to call home...we can do that. We can take care of the household of believers. And that will be something. Something truly amazing— another reason for people to look at the church and see the gospel of Christ made attractive.

Well, age has started showing up. Not just on me, but around me, too. Over the last few years I've lost some friends. Some of my influences have gone on to receive their reward.

Uncle Hank, who I always called Henry, even after he was made doctor, died of liver cancer. He was my guru, my friend, inventor of Pied Pipers, and I think of him every day.

And Calvin died.

Joyce, his wife, called me the day he had them turn off his IV, an electrolyte and nutrient cocktail meant to prolong his life. He was dying of cancer and had decided enough was enough. I told Joyce I'd wanted to see him one last time.

I hung up and not five minutes later the phone rang and it was Joyce again.

"Steve, can you come on down here now? I told Calvin you had plans to come see him."

"Yeah?" I said.

"He told them to start the IV back up!"

No one's ever postponed an appointment to get with me that meant so much. The Lord waited another day so Calvin and I could talk.

I think about dying every day. I have for as long as I can remember. For as long as I have memory, going back at least to two years old, I've believed in God. And for that long I've thought about dying at least once a day.

> Now I lay me down to sleep
>> I ask the Lord my soul to keep
> If I should die before I wake
>> I ask the Lord my soul to take.

Every day of my life, I've either said that prayer in earnest as a child or thought of it as an adult. Or said it with my kids.

I read a lot of Vonnegut in high school and college. I time travel in my head.

I think about the past easily.

I think about the future. I think about the fact that just as real as this breath is, this moment, so soon will be my last and the reality of standing before God. That's why I wanna hear him say, "Well done."

I can't begin to comprehend it. But I can read about it in the Bible, and imagine it in my heart and my nervous system.

Psychosomatics: the notion that your nervous system doesn't know the difference between a real experience and a strongly imagined experience. You know, like your heart can beat fast just remembering an embarrassing event, as if your body were going through it all over again.

Every day I imagine that moment when it's all over on this earth and time for the next.

Freaky, huh?

I feel sorry for people who won't even consider having faith in God and reading the Bible. As difficult as it may be to conceive of a God who loves you like a father, you've got to consider that it's as possible and plausible as anything. I've adopted a Pac-Man philosophy to help me overcome any doubts I face. Yeah, I have to battle doubts the same as the next guy. But most doubters are hoping that there isn't a God so nothing will really matter. When my faith gets weak, it's because I've only got half a brain. I can *pose* the really hard questions, but I can't answer them. That's where faith comes in and my Pac-Man theology.

The best man in my wedding, my best friend throughout my early life, was another guy named Steve. He told me one time that the easiest way to understand that you can't understand God is to imagine that you're Pac-Man in that video game of the same name. Imagine you're a one-dimensional video character and someone tries to convince you that there is life beyond what you can see. You just go along, wockah-wockah-wockah-wockah, and along comes someone trying to convince you that you were created by beings who put quarters into a big machine and make you move around going wockah-wockah-wockah—you'd think they were nuts. You'd have the same amount of difficulty believing in such a creator as...some folks have today believing in a Father who'd give his Son to die on a cross for our sins. But it's crazy not to consider it.

It's crazy to give your existence over to anarchy. Life without God doesn't work.

But it's equally crazy to believe in God and not accept the fact that he wants us to be saved.

I think too many people go to church and work and pray and study their Bibles and share their faith and still feel...lost. You know how it's wrong for people to believe that they're saved because they "feel" saved? What about our problem? The members who "feel" lost, even though God has promised them that they're saved. John says that he's writing so that we can "know that we are saved." What's the difference in having confidence in God and having faith in God? I can't see much difference.

True, Paul tells disciples that they must "work out their salvation with fear and trembling," but that's in the context of not becoming cocky and conceited; pride comes before the fall. But too many people are missing the peace that passes understanding. God loves us. Not capriciously, but earnestly. Tenderly. That's why we need to recycle our hearts and give them over to the Lord. Then trust that he will not throw them away.

Well, hope I didn't pop the illusionary bubble that if you could hang out with me you'd think you died and went to heaven. Lots of people have sent me mail saying that they wanted to spend the first days in heaven finishing the fellowship they've started that always gets interrupted. I've wondered if we'd read in heaven. Maybe we get to read and the time/space continuum works in such a way that the lives we live are the books we're reading in heaven at this very moment, or maybe the Web sites we're visiting there...right now....

Whoa, boy....Lassie come home.... Can you hear me, Major Tom?

Who knows?

God and only God, and he's tellin' only what you can read in his book.

I'm a lucky man. My family, most of 'em, are in the church. My dad, that sorry, good-for-nothing who hurt my mom back before I was born, well, he's a preacher on staff with the church in Atlanta, and he's my hero.

Every one of us are guilty of comparing ourselves to someone worse than us so as to feel better about ourselves. My dad always compared himself to his dad and brother. They were a coupla' Arkansas backwoods wildcats who thought that man was made to work hard and have sex every chance he got. Compared to them, my dad knew he was a gentleman of the highest order. It was not until he met the Lord that he began to compare himself to someone who would lead him to confess his double life and become a role model I'm proud to call "Dad."

Somewhere I read about an illustration to use in counseling where you imagine yourself over the jaws of hell and someone has to hold your hand for eternity or you'll fall in. They let go; you die.

My dad was born just before the Depression in the middle of nowhere. He was a runt, nearly died of scarlet fever and was given the name "Jockey" for both his size and my uncle's fondness of setting him on horses and cows and watching him ride.

One time, my uncle, his brother (four years his senior) and several redneck buddies, bent down a sapling and set dad on it and said, "Hold on!" They let go, and he flew up out of that tree, catapulting into a neighboring pine tree. He was a jockey all right.

*My Pawpaw's house*

But I see my dad as this little boy who wanted to be something. Not a poor farmer—a business man, someone who wore suits and ties and did important stuff.

I've seen the pictures, and sure enough, Dad was always dressed nicer than everyone around him. I know that my grandma wasn't good at cleaning and ironing and such. She'd fix dad's clothes for school and when she wasn't watching (which must have been a mean feat—they lived in a four-room shack—I'll show you the pictures sometime) he'd re-iron his shirts and slacks.

He was ashamed of his upbringing, and that set him up to lie about it. He always wanted to make himself look better, be better than he was.

But when I became a man, my dad told me his whole story. Things he'd done, wished he hadn't. Things he wished he could undo. And I realized how God worked in my family. The Lord had taken a coupla' Arkansas backwoods nobodies and given us an incredible life. I always thought I should be pumping gas somewhere. Instead, God used the shameful things to humble us and bring glory to him.

But having mentioned my grandpa, let me tell you something. It's time to go now, so don't worry, I'll tell you this story while we're walking to the car. I remember what the third grader said about Socrates: "He was a teacher. He talked a lot. They killed him."

We're finished. I've talked too much, and you've got to go, and I've got some other things to do myself. I haven't even told you about my garden projects and how I'll use 'em for missions contribution. Or about the stuff going on in Africa. I'll have to get on-line in a minute and write that stuff. Join me there. But now we gotta go. Just let me tell you about C. B. Johnson on the way out.

My grandpa was a sorry deal most of his life. At least when it came to morality. But he stopped drinking when he got married and worked his hands into calluses every bit as hard as the bottom of your shoes. I've seen him reach into a wasp's nest and pinch 'em all to death with his fingers.

His name was Cautis Basil Johnson. But nobody I heard ever called him that. He was Pawpaw to me and Daddy to my dad...till the day he died.

I was playing dominoes with that old man when I was fourteen in the summer of '69. We were playing while Armstrong walked on the moon. Grandpa didn't believe it was real. He thought TV wrestling was real, but he thought they faked the moon landing.

He couldn't read or write. One time a new cop stopped him for drunk driving. Grandpa wasn't drunk; he just kept pulling over on the two lane country road to let cars pass him when they pulled up behind him.

He'd been a bat out of hell driver my whole life. You could see grandpa's dust a mile away in his old '47 Ford that he drove like a kamikaze on speed. But in his last years he'd poke along at thirty-five and pull over on the shoulder to let cars pass. A new, young, town cop pulled him over.

"Okay you old wino, let me see your license."

My grandpa handed him his wallet.

"They're in there, officer. I don't know one piece of paper with writin' on it from another."

"Don't hand me that billfold; take your license out and show 'em to me, you dumb ole wino."

"Like I said, son, I don't know which one it is."

"Listen you..."

Grandpa took his wallet back.

"Suit yourself, boy," he said, putting his wallet in his pocket.

The sheriff pulled up.

"What's the problem?"

When grandpa told him what was going on, the wiser sheriff sent Pawpaw on home, informing the rookie that he'd just about made the stupidest mistake in his short career. Everyone in Monroe County knew grandpa hadn't had a drink in about sixty years.

Once I was with Pawpaw at Mr. Deaton's store. He'd take me there to get cho-chos—that's what he called chocolate-covered vanilla ice cream on a stick. And peanuts. We'd put peanuts, salted ones, in our RCs and drink 'em.

Pawpaw cussed in front of me, joking about something off-color and then quickly added, "I'm sorry, son. Don't mind me. I'm just playin' the fool."

"Playin' the fool." That's what he'd say when he knew he'd gone too far with something in front of his church-going grandson. "Don't mind me. I'm just playin' the fool."

Two years ago I was walking in my backyard with a handful of something. My mom and dad were visiting, and my dad said, "You walk just like my daddy used to."

I guess genetics are strong. I've got a lot of my grandpa in me, like it or not. And who'd know better than my dad? My dad, Jockey Johnson, the man I'd want to hold my hand if I was stuck over the pit of hell, because I know long after his strength gave out, he'd never let go. His love would lock his bones and he'd rot before he'd let go of his son.

And I know what I'm talking about because now I'm a dad, too.

Pete Rose said he'd walk through hell in a gasoline suit to play baseball. The only thing that I feel that passionately about now is getting my kids to

*C. B. Johnson, my grandfather, playing dominoes with me around the winter of '73, just after my grandmother died that September.*

heaven. Not that I intentionally love them more than the Lord. But by loving them the way I do, it makes me mindful of everything I do: my example in evangelism, in attitude, in faith, speech and purity.

I was sitting at the kitchen table with McCall a coupla' years ago. She was eight and I was trying to explain to her how I thought that I was messing up as a disciplinarian.

"I'm afraid the Lord is probably not pleased with me."

"What do you mean?" she asked.

"Well, I don't think I discipline you enough. Like I should."

She looked puzzled, so I added, "You know, it says in the Bible 'spare the rod, spoil the child.'"

She shot back bullet quick, "Yeah, but you know, that could mean, 'Spare the rod! *Spoil* the child!'" She was saying it like it was a command of the Lord God Almighty: Thou shalt spare that rod; ye must spoil that child!

I realized that, without a lot of help, I was raising a Baptist seminarian.

So, I see raising children as holding their little hands for their whole lives as they dangle over the jaws of hell. Oh, I know that Jesus has 'em on his lap, and thank God the angels are on constant guard duty.

Please. But I have to act like it's all up to me, even though I'm begging the Lord and my elders to help me all the time. And after all, the only things that I've got a shot at being the best in the world at are best husband for Lisa and best father for McCall and Skylar—they are also the only thing I can totally blow and not be able to make up for later.

And I'm not a good dad. At least not a naturally good parent. I'm not begging for arguments here: "No, Steve, you're a leader in the church; you're awesome; and you're an awesome dad...."

I'd be a great schoolmate, playmate, buddy, pal...dog. But it's very hard for me to be the parent. That's why I call Sheridan and Debbie Wright almost every day. They keep me from letting my emotional, rash or easy-going nature control me, and I've never in my life asked for help like I do with my kids. I'm holding 'em over hell, in my mind, remember, and I want some help.

And these are great kids.

We went to an orphanage in Soweto where all the babies are HIV-positive. McCall and Skylar held the babies, wanted to adopt them all. We go to orphanages in almost every country we visit, and when McCall was just five, she wanted to adopt Omar Moody, a little boy in Jamaica she held and couldn't let go of. And when it came time to leave the Soweto orphanage, a caretaker took Lisa aside and said, "You need to have your children wash their hands now, since they've touched the babies."

Discreetly Lisa took McCall and Skylar to a sink in another room to wash their hands...after we'd pried them away from the infants. McCall looked a little confused at first, then somber. We went to the car and drove away and she stared silently out the window as we passed the tin-roofed shanties.

With a voice that sounded too old and tired—a voice that had seen too much to be just seven and American—McCall told us as she stared out the window, "Usually you have to wash your hands *before* you hold a baby..." then she looked tearfully into Lisa's eyes and added, "...not *after.*"

So maybe she gets it. And will help us help Skylar get it.

And maybe I'm doing the right thing. You see, I used to think that I needed to invest in my children's future. Now I think I need to *invest them in the future.* I'm trying to expose them to everything I can in the church—evangelism, benevolence, Bible study, friendships—hoping that if they do it now, it will always be their favorite thing. Train a child in the way he should go... (Proverbs 22:6).

Ask McCall what her favorite thing is, and she'll say "going to church." It would be nice if she made a dean's list some day, but it's imperative that she makes the Lord's list on Judgment Day.

Now all I care about is the Lord saying, "Well done good and faithful servant" to my babies. I just wanna hear him say, "Well done" to them.

"Well done, good and faithful servant. Well done, McCall. Well done, Skylar. Enter into the reward I've prepared for you since before the beginning of time. Come to my house tonight and never leave, never cry, never have to wash your hands again; never be hungry or sad or lonely again; where everything is fair and my love and grace and goodness and mercy shall follow you forever."

That will be cool. I just wanna hear him say, "Well done" to my girls.

And to my girl...Lisa.

"Well done, Lisa, good and faithful servant....."

In spite of that idiot you married.

I just want to hear him say, "Well done" to my loved ones, my friends. My mom.

And to my daddy.

And okay, alright...I want to hear him say it to you, too.

If that means talking your ear off, so be it. 'Cause I'm like my grandpa. I'll be playin' the fool. Yes, siree, I'll play the fool and anything else I have to do if it's gonna help me hear him say, "Well done" to the sorry likes of all of us.

I'll be playin' the fool just like my Pawpaw. Just like that old guy I never, ever heard called by his real name, Cautis Basil.

Everyone who loved him called him Uncle Scrub.

# Epilogue

First time I remember seeing the word "epilogue" was at the end of the TV show *The Fugitive*. I'm happy to report that in spite of writing this book, I'm not on the run and still seem to be in the good graces of all my friends.

The last few weeks I've been writing on the Internet, and as most of you know, when you get an email address, it's kinda like a license plate. Some people get a cool one, like a vanity plate. Most of us just get one that looks like spilt alphabet soup. When I first got my email account, I had a "luck of the draw," gobbledy-goop, no-fun name 'cause all my first choices, cool names like Ace or Mad-dog or Skywalker, had already been used, and now you could only get those with series numbers after them—and let's face it, who wants to be Ace2485099? Then I found out no one had Uncle Scrub as an address. So I became unclescrub@aol.com.

Uncle Scrub was my grandpa. No one living, not even my dad, knows why he was called that. The sheriff who pulled up the day the young cop was calling Paw-paw a wino...first words out of his mouth were, "What's wrong Uncle Scrubby? You okay?"

He lived in a four-room wooden shack built flat on the ground with no foundation and a corrugated tin roof all my life. My dad built a house beside him, and I was five before we had indoor plumbing. I was four-teen before my grandpa had indoor plumbing.

He heated his house with a cast iron wood stove that burned mostly the wooden slats of reject flooring from a nearby hardwood floor factory. And he had x-ray vision. He could see through the backs of domi-noes and tell you what you were holding.

Grandpa died the year after we started the church in New York, 1984. He survived my grandma by eleven years, and I must say, he wasn't a very religious man. But I loved him and I get a kick out of it when my dad says I do something that reminds him of my grandpa. Even if that means I just got caught "playin' the fool."

We all like to know where we came from. I don't know why, and since you already know that I could waste pages pondering the subject, I'll just say that since the Bible goes into such great detail on the ori-gins of man, maybe God instilled in us a need to know whence we came.

I was born in a hamlet barely big enough to be called a town and grew up in the middle of a soybean field in a community named Bethlehem. Most of my friends were farmers who lost their farms and ended up doing odd jobs all their lives. Our glory days were destined to be a few moments in high school of playing football, and I was surely marked for a simple existence and humble circumstances. But God likes farmers and shepherds and stuff.

That Kip ever wanted me to be with him and that Lisa ever married me, that I ever even got to see, much less live in and lead the church in New York City, seems like a practical joke that God played on Satan. I can just hear the devil screaming, "It's not fair! I coulda' taken that pip-squeak out anytime! Who' would've thought he'd ever be useful for anything! He's supposed to be on a tractor, drinking Jack Daniels and losing the farm!" God always gets the last, and loudest, laughs.

That's how God brought the church into the world. Man waiting on some physical, earthly and powerful kingdom. God washes sins away in the waters of baptism, and 3,000 people begin the kingdom. What a joker, the Lord God Almighty. Always able to use the simple, plain and little, and sometimes weak, things to accomplish his will.

I'm so thankful just to be part of the church. Why God has seen fit to let me do what I do is a wonder to

*"This is my beloved, and this is my friend."*

me. In the last month and a half, I've been around the world, met the President twice (he remembered me and called me by name the second time), seen one of my best friends restored, written a book and directed the talent show at my kid's school. Only the talent show racked my nerves.

We're in a remarkable time. We're in a fellowship of churches that have grown from one congregation to 360 in 153 nations around the world. We have so many people and influences to thank for what God has accomplished through us, but if it hadn't been for the dedication of Kip and his family, we could easily have been like any other splintered sect scattered in the annals of church history. In a few short months, Lord willing, we will have accomplished our first goal, which is to establish churches in all the key cities of the world, over 170 nations when it's achieved. In June of next year we hope to celebrate this dream come true and when the party's over, go back to work, striving to do the rest of what Jesus has told us to do.

The biggest problems facing us are the results of shallow theology masquerading as zeal. We've got to be more than the people who always invite people to church. Our lives, as the old saying goes, have to back up our message. We've got to inspire and teach people how to live, how to follow in the footsteps of Jesus. I daresay we'll get much more persecution for moving people to be like Jesus than we ever have from inviting college students to small group Bible studies. We should shudder to think what will happen if we neglect our children or fail to take care of the poor who are "inside" the church. No, we need to stop shuddering and shoulder the work of raising kids who will find in the church the most glorious life possible. We must shoulder the work of taking care of the poor in our fellowship, so that no one ever goes without a roof over their head if Christ is their head. They're our family and we'll be worse than infidels if we don't take care of our family.

So, we need to see the rest of our lives not as either/or. Evangelism isn't what we do—it's who we are. We can't stop focusing on sharing our faith to meet the other needs in our churches. And we can't neglect those needs, either. We've got to follow and imitate Jesus more closely and remember that he did *all things* well.

The problems we face aren't what some think. We're not a cult. Unless being followers of Jesus and believers in the Bible makes you a cult. We respect and love our leaders, but we've stepped down leaders from every level if they have disqualified themselves. We don't blindly follow men. Christ is our king. We follow men and women as they follow Christ, but not as automatons mindlessly being duped by mortals for personal gain. We follow anyone who seems to lead us in a more Christlike direction and forgive those who fall, even if they were supposed to be out front leading us faithfully. We pick them up, and we'll carry each other to the pearly gates if need be.

And we're not failing. True, many have become discouraged and left our congregations. But the movie ain't over yet. And in spite of the losses, we're still expanding in numbers, numbers of members and numbers of congregations. Every ten minutes or less, someone is getting baptized somewhere in our fellowship. And every week, another congregation is getting started. What we have to accept as individual disciples is that it's leadership's job to equip the church to do the work of the ministry and all of our jobs, our lots in life, to not grow weary in doing good. We must not get tired of doing the same good things over and over again. That's what it means to be steadfast, unmovable.

I hope this book has helped. If you're reading this part, then you've stuck with me for a while. I hope it's not because you're still waiting for me to say something worthwhile. I hope it's because you enjoyed the company. I'm not a scholar or a theologian. I can read and I talk a lot, so I became a preacher. In spite of my self-deprecating manner, I did have a few other choices in life. But the words of Paul wouldn't stop ringing in my ears: "Woe to me if I preach not the gospel."

Early on, I wanted to be nothing but a preacher and in pursuing that desire, I've had opportunities I'd never have dreamed of. Maybe that's what Jesus meant when he said "no one who's left home or brothers or sisters or mother or father or children or fields for me and the gospel will fail to receive a hundred times as much in this present age...." A hundred times. At least.

If you do one thing long enough, you might be able to get good at it. As different as we all are, we all bring something to the party. Our strength is best seen when we do one thing in a united effort. If I can move you to join me in one desire, a common craving that maybe will compel us all to do what's right, then let it be this: Want, more than anything in life, want to hear the Lord say, "Well done, good and faithful servant."

C. S. Lewis said something about how it's only those Christians who think most about heaven who have any impact on earth. Join with me. Let's stop worrying about people thinking that our faith is just a crutch. Stop fretting about that old saying that went something like "pie in the sky by and by." Few alive today even remember such things. Heaven is one of the greatest motivators ever. Hell's a good one, too.

Let's decide to live for eternity and long to hear him say, "Well done."

He won't say it complimenting our perfection. We'll never be perfect. And he won't say it because we deserve it. We'll never deserve it.

He'll say it because we're his children and he loves us. Fathers love to praise their children. And who knows? It may be just the encouragement we need for our next adventure, one only the Lord knows anything about.

**DISCIPLESHIP
PUBLICATIONS
INTERNATIONAL**

# Who Are We?

Discipleship Publications International (DPI) began publishing in 1993. We are a nonprofit Christian publisher affiliated with the International Churches of Christ, committed to publishing and distributing materials that honor God, lift up Jesus Christ and show how his message practically applies to all areas of life. We have a deep conviction that no one changes life like Jesus and that the implementation of his teaching will revolutionize any life, any marriage, any family and any singles household.

Since our beginning we have published more than 75 titles; plus we have produced a number of important, spiritual audio products. More than one million volumes have been printed, and our works have been translated into more than a dozen languages—international is not just a part of our name! Our books are shipped regularly to every inhabited continent.

To see a more detailed description of our works, find us on the World Wide Web at www.dpibooks.com. You can order books or request a catalog by calling 1-888-DPI-BOOK twenty-four hours a day. From outside the US, call 781-937-3883, ext. 231 during Boston-area business hours.

We appreciate the hundreds of comments we have received from readers. We would love to hear from you. Here are other ways to get in touch:

Mail: DPI, One Merrill St., Woburn, MA 01801

Email: dpibooks@icoc.org

# Find us on the
# World Wide Web

www.dpibooks.com

1-888-DPI-BOOK

outside US: 781-937-3883 x231